TH

C

ENGLISH DICTIONARY

CONCISE ENGLISH DICTIONARY

Editor:

Martin H. Manser

Assistant Editors:

Stephen Curtis

David Pickering

Emma Redfern

English Trust
Downwood
Claverton Down Road
Bath
England
BA2 6DT

Printed in China

In the Concise English Dictionary you will find the following:

Thoughts from a Dyslexic Publisher

What a waste!

When I left school, my headmaster gave me a piece of paper to confirm I was no longer a schoolboy and ready to be sent out into the big wide world. As he handed me the certificate, he said to me in a soft voice, "What a waste!" This was not the most encouraging words for a boy of fifteen, in school for the last time, facing with trepidation the adult world.

"What a waste!" ... I was born in the city slums during a bombing raid on 26th February 1941, with dyslexia and a severe tongue tie that was not rectified until I had started work as an errand boy for a 'Family Grocer'.

An operation

While I was an errand boy, unable to communicate with other staff in the shop, Mrs. Siddall an ex-nurse, (now working in the shop) discovered that I was tongue-tied. Within a short period of time, I found myself in an operating theatre with a tall surgeon surrounded by a team of medical students examining and discussing my condition.

The surgeon wanted the students to witness my difficulty in talking.

He invited me to recite the letters of the alphabet. To say I was embarrassed is a gross understatement: I simply did not know the alphabet. To communicate with the surgeon or to answer the students' questions was another impossibility. Happily the surgeon quickly appreciated the situation and relieved my humiliation.

Following the operation - which I am pleased to say was successful – the surgeon encouraged me to copy out a book by hand as well as to read it out loud. This is not the place to share in detail how I followed that advice, and the consequences of so doing. That has been told in my autobiography, "A Child Cries" and "The Miracle Book".

Your Editor – Martin Manser

However, what I can say is that I wished someone also had given me a dictionary – not a heavy resource or reference work – but something that I hope this work edited by Martin Manser proves to be to many.

My reason for inviting Martin Manser to edit this project was because of the high esteem in which he is held for his editing of numerous reference books and dictionaries from various reputable publishers. I am grateful that he and his associate editors have been willing to work on this project and understand the individual groups that I had in mind.

Slow learners

(1) This is a dictionary for the 'slow learners'. There are many individuals who never want to stop learning, but the process for them is a slow one. I do hope that the user-friendly approach in the page layout will be an encouragement to such a group.

Unconfident readers

(2) The 'unconfident readers'. There are many individuals who have lost confidence in reading for a variety of reasons. I do hope they will find this book becomes a guide and stimulates them to start reading again.

Poor spellers

(3) The 'poor spellers'. I am told this group is far larger than may at first be imagined.

As Martin himself has said to me, "Even the professionals from time to time need help in this direction."

I am pleased that we have included over 50 special 'Help Boxes' to help all of us who have difficulty with spelling.

Dyslexic friends

(4) Dyslexic friends. Being dyslexic myself I know that in all walks of life – from successful businessmen to those involved in the media, from 'celebrities' to those

whose names are unknown outside their immediate circle – being dyslexic is a genuine problem.

The thoughtful way that our Designer, Steve Carroll has interpreted the needs of dyslexic people I hope will be a great help. Steve, Martin and I are grateful for the advice and help we have received from dyslexic associations.

I constantly meet parents who have one child or grandchild with dyslexic problems of one kind or another. They have not been forgotten; this Dictionary is for them.

Children and Students

(5) School Children and Students. In more recent days, I have enjoyed the privilege of becoming an Ambassador for Birmingham University and expressing my concern for individuals from disadvantaged backgrounds who now have an opportunity to move to higher education. Not only that group, but all children and students can benefit from making this Dictionary their regular companion.

Of course, there is a whole range of Dictionaries which the wise student will make use of – and I likewise use them and commend them. But they tend to be 'resource' and 'reference' books. We desire that this "Really Useful Dictionary" will be a friend for life.

Overseas visitors

(6) Overseas Visitors. For all to whom English is a second language,
I hope this Dictionary will be of great help.

Mobile phone users

(7) Users of Mobile Phones and Computers. Many young people are developing a 'shorthand' English to 'text' messages. This Dictionary is for them too. This is why we have produced not only the standard editions, but also a 'Mobile English Dictionary'. Perhaps the culture of poor spelling encouraged by regular 'texting', could also become diluted by familiarity with this 'Really Useful English Dictionary'.

As you can see, a great deal of thought has gone into this Dictionary and my only regret is that I did not produce it 30 years ago, when I first entered publishing.

English Trust

In closing, I would like you to know that profits from the sale of this Dictionary are not going to Shareholders, but into the "English Trust" for the benefit of folk disadvantaged by dyslexia and reading problems.

Robert Hicks, Dyslexic Publisher

Section Notes

Section Notes

Section Notes

Before you start... to help you make the most of this dictionary

The aims of this dictionary

This book has been designed as a simple guide to the spelling of the more commonly used English words. Sometimes people say that they first need to know how a word is spelled before they can find it in the dictionary. We understand this and we have included special helps to tell you about the different ways in which English sounds are spelled to help you find the word in a dictionary.

We all need help

If you are not very good at spelling or if English is not your native language, then we hope that this dictionary will be useful to you. Even the most confident speakers and writers of English sometimes stumble over difficult spellings or find themselves uncertain about the right word. Somewhat ironically, much modern electronic communication – including email and mobile-phone text messaging – depends chiefly on the written word, making spelling important in using such systems. The rules of grammar and spelling may be considered less important in the age of the computer and mobile phone but the more users of such technology diverge from accepted practice, the greater is the risk of misunderstanding.

How many words are there in English?

There may be as many as two million words in the English language, depending on what you count as a word. No one knows for sure how many words an average speaker of English includes in his or her personal vocabulary, but estimates range from 10,000 to 12,000 words for a 16-year-old to between 20,000 and 60,000 for a college graduate. William Shakespeare, it has been calculated, used between 18,000 and 25,000 words in his various writings. With such a rich choice in even the most limited vocabulary, misspellings and misinterpretations appear to be inevitable. In this dictionary, we have included about 5,000 of the most frequently used words in English.

How do I find the word I am looking for?

All the main entry words are given in alphabetical order. The alphabet is given as guide letters on the right-hand pages. So if you are looking for a word beginning with **M**, you will see that this is about halfway through the alphabet.

At the top of each set of two pages are the first and last main entry word on those pages. These will help you find the word.

The word you are looking for may be a main entry word, for example, **mountain** or it may be one of the word-family words in *italics*, for example, *mountainous*. If you have difficulty knowing how to spell a word then you can use the special helps which tell you about how a sound may be spelled.

How is an entry arranged?

Each entry begins with the main entry word in **bold** on a new line. Then comes the definition on a new line, which is a short statement of what the word means. The definition does not include every meaning of the word, but is a guide to the word's main meaning. On the next line come some undefined words in *italics*. These are part of the 'word family' of the main entry word.

There is any important rule to remember about the order of the undefined words. If the main entry word is a noun and its plural is irregular, or if there might be doubt about what the plural form is, the plural is given first. All other undefined words are then listed in alphabetical order:

child
young person; boy or girl
children childhood childish childlike

Different spellings

Some words can be spelled in more than one way, but only the most common spellings are included here. If there are two widely-used alternatives then both are included, with the preferred standard form given first.

Different main entry words

Some main entry words have a small raised number after them:

fit[1]
suitable; ready; healthy; to make suitable for
fitted fitter fittest fitting

fit[2]
sudden attack or convulsion
fitful

This means that the main entry words are spelled the same but have different histories and are best thought of as different words.

All those who have helped compile this book hope that it will help you improve your spelling, increase your vocabulary and develop your ability to communicate more confidently.

Martin H. Manser

Abbreviations

Brit	British English
esp.	especially
fem.	feminine
masc.	masculine
pl.	plural
sing.	singular
US	American English

Section Notes

Text Abbreviations

Learn to express your text message the fastest and shortest way possible by using Text abbreviations. Here are the most popular 'SMS shortcuts' that will help you text quickly.

121	One To One
2U	To You
2U2	To You To
24/7	24 hours a day, 7 days a week

AAMOF	As A Matter Of Fact
AISE	As I Said Earlier
AISI	As I See It
AIUI	As I Understand It
AIW	As It Were
AND	Any Day Now
AFAICT	As Far As I Can Tell
AFAIK	As Far As I Know
AFAIR	As Far As I Remember
AOB	Any Other Business
ASL	Age Sex Location
AKA	Also Known As
AMAP	As Much As Possible
ASAP	As Soon As Possible
ATB	All The Best
ATM	At The Moment
AWCIGO	And Where Can I Get One?
AYT?	Are You There?
AYL	At Your Leisure

BBL	Be Back Later
B/C	Because

BC	Busy
B4	Before
BFN	Bye For Now
BB4N	Bye Bye For Now
BBIAM	Be Back In A Minute
BBL	Be Back Later
BCC	Blind Carbon Copy
BIL	Brother In Law
BION	Believe It Or Not
BOL	Best Of Luck
BRB	Be Right Back
BTA	But Then Again
BTM	Beats Me
BTW	By The Way
BWL	Bursting With Laughter
BZY	Busy

CUL8R	See You Later
C&G	Chuckle and Grin
CB	Call Back
CIAO	Goodbye
CIO	Cut It Out
CMIIW	Correct Me If I'm Wrong
CRAT	Can't Remember A Thing
CU	See You
CWYL	Chat With You Later
CYA	See Yah
CYO	See You Online

DAMHIK	Don't Ask Me How I Know
DIKU?	Do I Know You?
DIY	Do It Yourself
DTRT	Do The Right Thing

EB	Eye Ball
EMFBI	Excuse Me For Butting In
EMSG	Email Message
EOB	End Of Business

EOD	End Of Discussion
EOM	End Of Message
ESP	Specially
ETA	Estimated Time of Arrival

F2F	Face To Face
FAQ	Frequently Asked Question
FCFS	First Come First Served
FCOL	For Crying Out Loud
FOAF	Friend Of A Friend
FOS	Freedom Of Speech
FTBOMH	From The Bottom Of My Heart
FTR	For The Record
FWIW	For Whatever Its Worth
FYA	For Your Amusement
FYI	For Your Information

G2G	Got To Go
GA	Go Ahead
GAL	Get A Life
GF	Girl Friend
GFN	Gone For Now
GHM	God Help Me
GHY	God Help You
GIGO	Garbage In Garbage Out
GJ	Good Job
GL	Good Luck
GLYSDI	God Loves You and So Do I
GMT	Greenwhich Mean Time
GMTA	Great Minds Think Alike
GOI	Get Over It
GOWI	Get On With It
GR8	Great
GSM	God Save Me
GSH	Good Sense Of Humour

GTBOS	Glad To Be Of Service
GTG	Got To Go
GTGN	Got To Go Now
GTRM	Got To Read Mail
GTSY	Glad To See You

H2	How To
HAND	Have A Nice Day
HAGN	Have A Good Night
HHIS	Hanging Head In Shame
HHOK	Ha Ha Only Kidding
HICA	Here It Comes Again
HOAS	Hold On A Second
HSIK	How Should I Know
HP	Home Page
HTH	Hope This Helps
HH	Holding Hands

IAC	In Any Case
IAE	In Any Event
IAY	I Adore You
IAYT	I Adore You Too
IB	I'm Back
IC	I See
ICBW	I Could Be Wrong
ICCL	I Couldn't Care Less
IDN	I Don't Know
IDTS	I Don't Think So
IKWUM	I Know What You Mean
IOU	I Owe You
ILU	I Love You
ILU2	I Love You Too
ILU4E	I Love You Forever
IME	In My Experience
IMHO	In My Humble Opinion

IMO In My Opinion

INPO In No Particular Order

IOW In Other Words

IRL In Real Life

ISTM It Seems To Me

ISTR I Seem To Remember

ITYM I Think You Mean

IWALY I Will Always Love You

IWIK I Wish I Knew

IYKWIM If You Know What I Mean

IYSWIM If You See What I Mean

J/K Just Kidding

JAM Just A Moment/Minute

JFF Just For Fun

JFYI Just For Your Information

JIT Just In Time

JIC Just In Case

JLY Jesus Loves You

JMO Just My Opinion

JMHO Just My Humble Opinion

JTLYK Just To Let You Know

JTYMLTK Just Thought You Might Like To Know

KIA Know It All

KISS Keep It Simple Stupid

KIT Keep In Touch

KOTC Kiss On The Cheek

KOTL Kiss On The Lips

KWIM Know What I Mean

KYHU Keep Your Head Up

L8R Later

L8R G8R Later Alligator

LALL	Live And Let Live
LHM	Lord Help Me
LHY	Lord Help You
LHU	Lord Help Us
LJBF	Let's Just Be Friends
LMA	Leave Me Alone
LMK	Let Me Know
LOL	Laughing Out Loud
LTBF	Learn To Be Funny
LTNS	Long Time No See
LTM	Laughing To Myself
LYWAMH	Love You With All My Heart

M8	Mate
MAY	Mad About You
MB	Message Board
MIL	Mother In Law
MPH	Miles Per Hour
ML	More Later
MOD	Master Of Disaster
MORF	Male Or Female
MOTOS	Member Of The Opposite Sex
MOTD	Message Of The Day
MYOB	Mind Your Own Business

N/M	Never Mind
NAGI	Not A Good Idea
NBD	No Big Deal
N/A	Not Applicable
NE1	Anyone
NLT	Not Later Than
NM	Never Mind
NMP	Not My Problem
NMS	Not My Style
NOYB	None Of Your Business
NP	No Problem

NTG	Not To Good
NYP	Not Your Problem
OIC	Oh I See
ONNA	Oh No Not Again
OTOH	On The Other Hand
OTTOMH	Off The Top Of My Head
PCB	Please Call Back
PDS	Please Don't Shout
PLS	Please
PM	Private Message
PCAHF	Put On A Happy Face
PPL	People
PRW	People/parents are watching
PTL	Praise the Lord
PXT	Please Explain That
PU	That Stinks
QIK	Quick
RL	Real Life
RME	Rolling My Eyes
ROTFL	Rolling On The Floor Laughing
RSN	Real Soon Now
SICNIZ	Sorry I Could Not Resist
SIG2R	Sorry I Got To Run
SMHID	Scratching My Head In Disbelief
SOMY	Sick Of Me Yet?
SPK	Speak
SPST	Same Place, Same Time
SOTMG	Short Of Time, Must Go
SS	So Sorry
SSDD	Same Stuff Different Day
SSINF	So Stupid It's Not Funny

STR8	Straight
STW	Search The Web
SUITM	See You In The Morning
SUL	See You Later
SUP	What's Up?
SYL	See You Later

TA	Thanks A Lot
TAFN	That's All For Now
TAM	Tomorrow a.m.
TBH	To Be Honest
TC	Take care
TGIF	Thank God It's Friday
THX	Thanks
TIA	Thanks In Advance
TIAD	Tomorrow Is Another Day
TLK2UL8R	Talk To You Later
TMI	Too Much Information
TMWFI	Take My Word For It
TNSTAAFL	There's No Such Thing As A Free Lunch
TPM	Tomorrow p.m.
TPTB	The Powers That Be
TTFN	Ta Ta For Now
TTTT	These Things Take Time
TTYL	Talk To You Later
TTYS	Talk To You Soon
TU	Thank You
TY	Thank You
TYT	Take Your Time
TYVM	Thank You Very Much

UGTBK	You've Got To Be Kidding
UKTR	You Know That's Right
UL	Upload
UR	Your/You're

UV	Unpleasant Visual
WAM	Wait A Minute
WAN2TLK	Want To Talk
WAYF	Where Are You From?
WB	Welcome Back
WIIFM	What's In It For Me?
WK	Week
WKD	Weekend
WTG	Way To Go
WU?	What's Up?
WUF?	Where Are You From?
WWJD	What Would Jesus Do?
WWYC	Write When You Can
WYSIWYG	What You See Is What You Get
YBS	You'll Be Sorry
YGBKM	You Gotta Be Kidding Me
YMMV	Your Mileage May Vary
YW	You're Welcome

THE REALLY USEFUL ENGLISH DICTIONARY

Aa

a
indefinite article, used before consonant sounds

aback (taken aback)
startled

abandon
to give up; to forsake
abandonment

abbreviate
to make shorter
abbreviating abbreviation

ability
skill or power to do something
abilities

able
with the skill or power to do something
abler ablest ably

abnormal
different from the normal
abnormality abnormalities

abolish
to do away with
abolishes abolition

abortion
removal or expulsion of a foetus from the womb
abort abortive

about
concerning; near; around; approximately

above
at a higher or greater point

abroad
in or to a foreign country

absent
not present; away from
absence absentee

absolute
complete; perfect; unlimited
absolutely

absorb
to take in; to suck up
absorbent absorption

abstract
not material; not depicting a person or object; summary
abstraction

abuse
to use wrongly or improperly; to treat cruelly; to insult; insulting language
abusive

academic
theoretical; scholarly
academically

academy
institution; school
academies

accelerate
to increase speed
accelerating acceleration accelerator

accent
distinctive pronunciation; emphasis; written mark
accentuate

accept
to receive; to agree to
acceptability acceptable acceptably acceptance

access
right to approach or use
accesses accessibility accessible

accessory
useful additional part
accessories

accident
unexpected chance event
accidental

accommodate
to provide with lodging; to do a favour for
accommodating accommodation

accompany
to go along with; to play a supporting musical part
accompanied accompanies accompaniment accompanying

according
in relation (to); as said or shown by
accordingly

account
statement of finances; (to give a) description or explanation
accountability accountable accountancy accountant

accumulate
to collect; to gather together
accumulating accumulation

accurate
correct; exact
accuracy

accuse
to charge someone with a particular crime
accusation accuser accusing

ache
(to suffer from a) continuous dull pain
aching

achieve
to succeed in doing
achievement achiever achieving

acid
sour; chemical compound
acidity

acknowledge
to admit; to recognize
acknowledgement or acknowledgment acknowledging

acquaint
to make familiar (with)
acquaintance

acquire
to gain possession of
acquiring acquisition acquisitive

acre
unit of area, 4840 square yards
acreage

across
from one side to the other of; on the other side of

act
deed; statute; main division of a play; to do something; to perform a part in a play, etc.

action
process of doing something; lawsuit

active
functioning; energetic
activity activities

actor (fem. **actress**)
person who acts in a play, film, etc.
actresses

actual
real
actually

adapt
to make suitable; to modify to fit
adaptability adaptable adaptation adapter or adaptor

add
to combine numbers into a total; to join

addition
adding
additional additive

address
written description of where a building is; to speak to
addresses addressee

adequate
sufficient; just satisfactory
adequacy

adjective
word used to describe a noun

adjourn
to postpone temporarily
adjournment

adjust
to change slightly; to adapt

administer
to direct, manage, or control; to dispense or give
administration administrative administrator

admire
to regard with great respect
admiring

admission
(charge for) admitting; confession

admit
to allow to enter; to acknowledge
admittance admitted admitting

adolescence
period between puberty and maturity
adolescent

adopt
to take, esp. a child, as one's own
adoption adoptive

adult
fully-developed and mature person
adulthood

advance
to go forwards
advancing

advantage
favourable position; gain, or benefit
advantageous

adventure
exciting or risky event, undertaking, etc.
adventurer adventurous

adverb
word describing how, when, where, etc., something is done

advertise
to present to the public in order to promote sales
advertisement advertiser advertising

advice
recommendation on action or behaviour

advise
to give advice to; to inform
advisable adviser or advisor advising advisory

advocate
person who speaks for another; supporter; to recommend
advocating

aerial
of, in, or from the air; rod or rods for transmitting or receiving radio waves

aeroplane
(US **airplane**)
aircraft

aerosol
(suspension of) fine particles sprayed from a pressurized container

affair
matter or concern; event; extramarital sexual relationship

affect
to influence; to move emotionally

affection
fondness
affectionate

afford
to have enough to be able to buy or do something

afraid
frightened; sorry

after
following in time or space; in the same way as
afterwards

afternoon
period between noon and evening

again
once more; further

against
opposing; in contact with; in preparation for

age
length of time a person or thing has existed; to grow old
aged ageing or aging ageism

agency
business providing a service; means
agencies

agenda
list of things to be considered

agent
person who acts for someone else; something that produces an effect

aggravate
to make worse; (*informal*) to annoy
aggravating aggravation

aggression
unprovoked attack
aggressive aggressor

agitate
to disturb or excite
agitating agitation agitator

ago
in the past

agony
extreme pain
agonies agonize or agonise

agree
to share the same opinion;
to assent (to);
to suit the health of
agreeable agreed agreeing agreement

ahead
in front; in the future

aid
(to give) help

aim
to point at; purpose

air
mixture of gases; manner; quality

aircraft
vehicle that flies through the air

airline
company that provides air travel

airport
place where aircraft land and take off

aisle
passageway between seats

alarm
(to give a) warning signal;
to frighten

album
book for collection of stamps, photographs, etc.; long-playing record

alcohol
clear intoxicating liquid
alcoholic alcoholism

alert
watchful; to warn

alibi
evidence of being somewhere else when a crime was committed; excuse
alibis

alien
foreign; not natural (to)
alienate

alight[1]
to come down from

alight[2]
on fire

alike
similar

alive
living; aware of

all
whole amount of; wholly

allege
to state without proof
allegation allegedly alleging

alley
narrow passage
alleys

alliance
union or association

allocate
to assign for a particular purpose
allocating allocation

allow
to permit
allowance

ally
to join with; country or ruler supporting another; supporter
allies allied allying

almost
very nearly

alone
apart from others

along
over the length of; onwards; accompanying
alongside

aloud
loud enough to be heard

alphabet
set of letters in a writing system
alphabetical

already
by or before a particular time

also
besides

alter
to change
alteration

alternate
(to occur) in turns; every other
alternating alternation alternator

alternative
giving or of a choice; possible choice
alternatively

although
even though

altogether
with everything considered; completely

always
at all times

am
1st person singular of present tense of be

amateur
not professional or expert
amateurish

amaze
to fill with wonder or surprise
amazing

ambassador
diplomatic representative to another country

ambiguous
having two or more possible meanings; doubtful
ambiguity ambiguities

ambition
strong desire for success
ambitious

ambulance
vehicle for transporting the sick and injured

amend
to change formally; to improve
amendment

amid
in the middle of
amidst

among or **amongst**
in the middle of; between

amount
(to) total

amphibian
animal that can live on land or in water
amphibious

ample
plentiful; large
amply

amplify
to make stronger
or louder;
to expand on
amplification amplified amplifier
amplifies amplifying

amuse
to entertain;
to cause to laugh
amusing

an
indefinite article, used before vowel sounds

anaesthesia
(US **anesthesia**)
loss of ability to feel, esp. pain
anaesthetic (US *anesthetic*)
anaesthetist (US *anesthetist*)
anaesthetize or *anaesthetise* (US *anesthetize*)

analyse (US **analyze**)
to examine in detail
analysing (US *analyzing*)

analysis
act or result of analysing
analyses analyst analytic analytical
analytically

anatomy
study of the structure of organisms
anatomic anatomical anatomically
anatomist

ancestor (fem. **ancestress**)
person from whom another is descended
ancestral ancestry

anchor
device that holds a ship firmly
to the sea-bed
anchorage

ancient
very old

and
in addition; also

angel
divine messenger
angelic angelically

anger
great annoyance

angle
space between lines extending from a common point

angry
very annoyed
angrier angriest angrily angriness

animal
living creature able to feel and move

ankle
joint connecting the foot
and leg

anniversary
date each year on which an event is celebrated
anniversaries

announce
to make known publicly
announcement announcer
announcing

annoy
to irritate or harass
annoyance

annual
yearly
annually

anonymous
by an unknown or unnamed author
anonymity

anorak
hooded waterproof jacket

another
additional or different
(person or thing)

answer
(to) reply; to take responsibility (for)

ant
kind of small insect

antibiotic
(substance) used to treat infection
with bacteria

anticipate
to expect; to see in advance and
prepare for
anticipating anticipation

antique
very old; old sought-after object
antiquate antiquity antiquities

antiseptic
(substance) that stops growth
of bacteria

anxiety
fear and worry
anxieties anxious

any
some; every

anybody
any person

anyhow
in any case; carelessly

anyone
anybody

anything
any object, event, etc.

anyway
in any case

anywhere
in, at, or to any place

apart
distant; separate

apartment
single room;
set of rooms;
(US) flat

ape
tailless monkey;
to imitate
aping

apologetic
being or saying sorry
apologetically

apologize or **apologise**
to say one is sorry
apologizing or *apologising*

apology
expression of regret
apologies

apostrophe
punctuation mark

appal (US **appall**)
to fill with horror, dismay, or shock
appalled appalling

apparent
clearly seen or understood
apparently

appeal
(to) request;
to be attractive (to)

appear
to come into sight
appearance

appendix
additional material at the end of a book; short, closed tube extending from large intestine
appendices or *appendixes*

appetite
desire, esp. for food
appetizer or appetiser *appetizing* or *appetising*

applaud
to show approval by clapping the hands
applause

apple
round edible fruit

apply
to put to use; to put into contact with; to request
applicable applicant application applied applies applying

appoint
to choose, esp. to do a job
appointee appointment

appraise
to assess the worth or quality of someone or something
appraisal

appreciate
to be grateful for; to recognize; to increase in value
appreciable appreciating appreciation appreciative

approach
to come near or nearer; method of doing something
approaches

appropriate
suitable; to take for one's own use
appropriating appropriation

approve
to think favourably of; to authorize
approval approving

approximate
nearly accurate or exact
approximation

apricot
round, orange-yellow fruit

April
4th month of the year

apron
protective garment; hard-surfaced area by airport terminal

apt
likely (to); suitable; clever
aptitude

aquarium
tank or pool in which fish, plants, etc., are kept
aquariums or *aquaria*

aquatic
living or found in water

arbitrary
chosen randomly and without reason
arbitrarily arbitrariness

arcade
covered passage; line of arches

arch
(to make into a) curved structure or shape

archaeology
(US **archeology**)
study of material remains of ancient human life
archaeological
(US *archeological*) *archaeologist*
(US *archeologist*)

archaic
of a remote period;
no longer used

architecture
science of designing buildings
architect architectural

archives
(place for storing) official records
archival archivist

are
plural of present tense of be

area
extent or expanse;
region or field

arena
enclosed area for sports events
arenas

aren't
(informal) are not

argue
to quarrel; to present reasons for or against something
arguable arguably arguing

argument
quarrel; reasons for or against something
argumentative

arise
to come into being
arisen arising arose

aristocracy
(government by the) privileged noble class
aristocracies aristocrat aristocratic aristocratically

arithmetic
branch of mathematics dealing with numbers
arithmetical

arm[1]
upper human limb

arm[2]
(to equip with a) weapon
armament

armour (US **armor**)
(to provide with a) defensive covering
armoured (US *armored*) *armourer* (US *armorer*) *armoury* (US *armory*) *armouries* (US *armories*)

army
military land forces of a country
armies

arose
past tense of **arise**

around
on all sides (of); approximately

arouse
to stimulate; to wake
arousal arousing

arrange
to put in order; to make plans for
arrangement arranging

arrest
to place in legal custody; to stop

arrive
to come to a destination
arrival arriving

arrogant
behaving in an aggressively proud way
arrogance

arrow
slender pointed weapon shot from a bow

art
skill; creative ability; painting, sculpture, etc.

artefact or **artifact**
man-made object

article
item or object; non-fiction writing in a newspaper

artificial
not natural; made by human skill
artificiality

artist
person who creates paintings, etc.
artistic artistically artistry

as
in or to the same degree or manner; like; in the role of; because

ash[1]
powder remaining after a fire
ashes ashen

ash[2]
tree of the olive family

ashamed
feeling shame

ashore
on or to land from water

aside
on or to one side

ask
to put a question to

asleep
sleeping

aspect
feature or appearance

aspirin
pain-relieving drug or tablet

assassin
someone who kills a famous person, esp. for political reasons
assassinate assassinating assassination

assault
(to make a) violent attack

assemble
to bring, come, or join together
assembling assembly assemblies

assert
to declare
assertion assertive

assess
to estimate or determine a value or amount
assesses assessment assessor

asset
valuable thing, quality, or person

assign
to choose or designate
assignation assignment

assimilate
to absorb
assimilating assimilation

assist
to help
assistance assistant

associate
to join or link; partner or colleague
associating association

assume
to suppose; to undertake
assuming assumption

assure
to make confident;
to promise; to insure
assurance assuring

astonish
to surprise greatly
astonishes astonishment

astrology
study of the influence of planets, etc., on human affairs
astrologer astrological

astronomy
study of stars and planets
astronomer astronomical

at
used to show position

ate
past tense of eat

athlete
person trained to compete in exercises or sports
athletic athletically athleticism athletics

atmosphere
air; environment or influence
atmospheric

atom
smallest particle of an element that takes part in chemical reactions
atomic

attach
to join or fasten
attaches attachment

attack
to act forcefully against; to start energetically on; strong hostile attempt

attempt
(to make an) effort

attend
to be present at;
to take care of
attendance attendant

attention
concentrated thought; awareness
attentive

attitude
mental position

attorney
person who has legal authority to act for another

attract
to be pleasing or desirable to; to pull or draw towards oneself
attraction attractive

attribute
to regard as due or belonging (to); quality
attributable attributing attribution

auction
public sale of goods or property to the highest bidder
auctioneer

audible
loud enough to be heard
audibility audibly

audience
group of people at a performance; formal interview

audio
(relating to) recorded sound

August
8th month of the year

aunt
sister of one's mother
or father; uncle's wife
(informal) auntie or aunty aunties

author
writer of a book, play, etc.
authorial authorship

authority
(person or organization that has the)
power or right to influence or control
authorities authoritarian authoritative

authorize or **authorise**
to give authority to;
to allow
authorization or *authorisation*
authorizing or *authorising*

automatic
working by itself; independent
automatically

autumn
season between summer and winter
autumnal

auxiliary
additional; (person or thing) providing
support
auxiliaries

available
able to be obtained, used, or reached
availability

avenue
broad street, often tree-lined

average
(to find the) result of adding
quantities and dividing by the number
of those quantities
averaging

avoid
to keep away from; to refrain from
avoidance

await
to wait for; to expect

awake
to wake; not sleeping
awaken awakening awaking awoke
awoken

award
to grant officially; prize

aware
having knowledge (of)

away
from one place; in another direction;
absent

awful
very great; (informal) unpleasant;
nasty
awfully

awkward
clumsy; difficult

awoke
past tense of awake

awoken
past participle of awake

axe (US **ax**)
tool for felling trees or chopping
wood; to cut with an axe
axing

Bb

baby
very young child
babies

bachelor
unmarried man; holder of lowest academic degree

back
rear part, esp. of body; to move away or in a reverse direction; to support
backward backwards

backbone
row of connected bones running along person or animal's back

background
part of a view far away; events that explain an event; person's origins or experience

bacon
cured meat from the side of a pig

bad
unpleasant; evil; decayed
badly

bade
past tense of **bid**[2]

badge
distinguishing emblem or mark

bag
(to put into a) flexible container
bagged bagging

baggage
luggage; equipment

bake
to cook by dry heat in an oven
baker bakery bakeries baking

balance
weighing device; (to bring or come into) equilibrium; difference between debits and credits
balancing

balcony
platform extending from a wall; theatre upper gallery
balconies

bald
without hair
balding

ball
round object, esp. used in games; social gathering for dancing

ballet
artistic dancing and mime to music; group of dancers
ballerina balletic

balloon
bag of light material that is filled with gas or air and floats in the air

ballot
secret voting; to vote

ban
to prohibit
banned banning

banana
kind of yellow, crescent-shaped fruit

band
group of people, esp. musicians; thin strip of material

bandage
(to cover with a) piece of material to dress a wound
bandaging

bang
(to make a) short loud explosive *noise*

bank
establishment for keeping, lending, etc., money; (to make into a) slope or mound; side of a river or lake

bankrupt
(a person who is) unable to pay his or her debts
bankruptcy bankruptcies

banner
flag

bar
long straight piece of something solid; counter; (to obstruct with a) barrier; to prohibit

barred
barring

barbecue
(to cook on an) outdoor grill
barbecued barbecuing

bare
naked, exposed; mere; to expose
barer barest baring

barely
only just; hardly

bargain
(to make an) agreement, esp. about a price; something bought cheaply

bark[1]
(of a dog) to make its typical cry

bark[2]
protective layer on a tree

barn
large farm building

barracks
buildings accommodating soldiers

barrel
(to put in a) cylindrical container; cylindrical part
barrelled (US *barreled*) *barrelling* (US *barreling*)

barrier
obstruction

barrister
lawyer who may plead in a higher court

base
bottom or supporting part; to establish
basing

basement
lowest part of a building

basic
fundamental
basically

basin
round open container, esp. for liquid

basis
foundation; main part
bases

basket
container made from interwoven pieces of cane, etc.

bat[1]
(to hit with a) wooden implement used in certain games
batted batting

bat[2]
nocturnal flying mammal

batch
(to put in a) group of similar things
batches

bath
(to wash in a) large container for washing the body

bathe
to swim; to immerse in water
bathing

bathroom
room where one can wash oneself; (US) toilet

batter[1]
to hit repeatedly and violently

batter[2]
mixture of flour, eggs, and milk or water

battery
electric cell or cells; group of guns
batteries

battle
(to) fight or struggle
battling

bay
wide inlet of sea, etc.; alcove or recess

be
to exist
am are been being is was were

beach
shore
beaches

beak
projecting horny part of bird's jaws

beam
long thick piece of wood; shaft of light

bean
kind of pod-bearing plant; seed of this

bear[1]
to carry; to show; to support; to give birth to
bore born borne

bear[2]
kind of large animal with shaggy coat

beard
hair growing on a man's face

beast
animal

beat
to hit repeatedly; to defeat; rhythm
beaten

beauty
qualities that delight the senses; good-looking person or thing
beauties beautiful beautifully

because
for the reason that

become
to come to be; to suit
became becoming

bed
place on which to sleep or rest; area of soil, esp. used for growing flowers
bedding

bedroom
room, containing a bed, in which someone sleeps

bee
4-winged insect that produces honey

beef
meat from cow, bull, etc.

been
past participle of be

beer
alcoholic drink

beetle
insect with hard front wings; to scurry

before
at an earlier time (than); in front of

beforehand
in advance

beg
to ask for money; to ask earnestly or humbly
beggar begged begging

begin
to perform the first part of
began beginner beginning *begun*

behalf
interest or part

behave
to act or function; to conduct oneself
behaving behaviour (US *behavior*)

behind
at the back (of); later than

being
present participle of be; existence; living creature

belief
feeling of certainty; something a person believes

believe
to accept as true; to think; to trust (in)
believing

bell
device that makes a ringing sound

belly
abdomen; stomach; to swell
bellies

belong
to be the property or possession (of)
belongings

below
at a lower level (than)

belt
band of leather, etc., worn round the waist

bench
long seat without a back; work-table
benches

bend
(to force or be forced into a) curve or turn
bent

beneath
below

beneficial
advantageous

beneficiary
person who benefits
beneficiaries

benefit
advantage; payment; to be useful or profitable to
benefited benefiting

bent
not straight; past tense and past participle of **bend**

bereave
to deprive of a person or thing, esp. by death
bereaved bereavement bereaving bereft

berry
small edible fruit
berries

beside
by the side of (a person or thing)

besides
in addition

best
of the most excellent, etc., kind

bet
money risked on the outcome of a contest; to place a bet
better or bettor betting

betray
to expose or show, esp. to an enemy; to be disloyal to
betrayal

better
of a more excellent, etc., kind; to make, become, or do better than

between
in the middle of (two things or people)

beware
to be cautious (of)

beyond
farther than

bias
(to) prejudice; tendency
biased or *biassed*
biasing or *biassing*

bicycle
(to ride a) 2-wheeled vehicle
bicycling

bid[1]
(to offer a) price at an auction; attempt
bidder *bidding*

bid[2]
to order
bade biddable bidden

big
large in size; important or powerful
bigger biggest biggish

bike
(informal) short for bicycle

bill[1]
statement of money owed; notice; proposed law

bill[2]
bird's beak

billion
thousand million; (formerly Brit) million million
billionaire billionth

a b c d e f g h i j k l m n o p q r s t u v w x y z

bin
container, esp. for waste; (informal) to throw away
binned binning

bind
to fasten together with rope, etc.
bound

binoculars
instrument that makes distant objects appear nearer

biography
account of a person's life
biographies biographer

biology
study of living organisms
biological biologist

bird
feathered animal

birth
process of being born; origin

birthday
day on which person was born

biscuit
small flat dry cake

bit[1]
small piece; basic unit of computer information

bit[2]
mouthpiece on horse's bridle; boring part of tool

bite
to cut or seize with the teeth
bit biting bitten

bitter
tasting sharp and unpleasant; resentful

black
completely dark; without light

blackboard
board for writing on with chalk

blade
cutting-part of a knife, etc.; flat wide part of an oar, etc.

blame
to hold someone responsible (for); responsibility for a fault
blameable or *blamable blaming*

blank
not written or printed on

blanket
thick covering on a bed; affecting everything or everyone equally; to cover with a thick layer of something
blanketed blanketing

blast
explosion; rush of wind; to produce a loud harsh noise

blaze
strongly burning flame; to burn strongly
blazing

bleach
to whiten, esp. chemically; whitening agent
bleaches

bleak
cheerless, gloomy

bleed
to lose or emit blood
bled

blend
(to make) a mixture

bless
to wish happiness; to make happy; to make holy
blessed or *blest* *blesses*

blew
past tense of **blow**[1]

blind
(to make) unable to see; cover for window; pretext

bliss
perfect happiness

block
large piece of wood, etc.; obstruction; to obstruct
blockage

blond (fem. **blonde**)
(person)
with fair hair

blood
red fluid circulating in the body

bloom
(to produce a) flower

blossom
(to produce) flowers on a plant, esp. a fruit tree

blouse
woman's shirt-like garment

blow[1]
to force a current of air
blew

blow[2]
powerful stroke; shock

blue
(to make or become the) colour of a clear sky
blueing or *bluing*
blueish or *bluish*

bluff
to deceive; an attempt to deceive

blunder
to make a mistake; to move clumsily

blunt
not sharp; direct

blur
to make or become unclear or vague
blurred *blurring*

blush
to become red from embarrassment, etc.
blushes

board
long flat piece of wood; group of people who supervise something; to go onto a ship, bus, etc.; (to be provided with) meals and lodging

boast
to speak about oneself proudly

boat
small vessel that travels over water

body
whole or main part of a human or animal; group
bodies *bodied* *bodily*

bog
marsh; to cause to sink, as if in a bog
bogged *bogging* *boggy*

boil[1]
to heat a liquid to a temperature at which it becomes vapour

boil[2]
inflamed swelling on the skin

boisterous
noisy and rough

bold
confident and courageous

bolt
(to lock with a) sliding bar to fasten a door; to move quickly

bomb
explosive device

bond
something that binds; a promise

bone
hard tissue forming the skeleton of an animal
bony

bonfire
large outdoor fire

bonnet
kind of hat; cover of a motor-vehicle engine

bonus
something extra that is given or paid
bonuses

book
printed pages bound together; to reserve

boom
to make a deep hollow sound; period of increased economic activity

boost
(to) increase

boot
strong shoe; luggage compartment in a car

booth
stall or small enclosure

border
(to form the) edge or boundary

bore[1]
past tense of **bear**[1]

bore[2]
to make a hole in wood, etc.
borer boring

bore[3]
(to make tired by being) dull and tedious
boredom boring

born
past participle of bear1; (brought into being) by birth; natural

borrow
to take temporarily on loan

boss
person in charge of or employing others; to give other people orders
bosses bossier bossiest bossily bossy

both
the 2

bother
to irritate; to care

bottle
(to put into a) narrow-necked container for liquids
bottling

bottom
lowest part of something

bought
past tense and past participle of buy

bounce
to spring back after hitting a surface suddenly
bouncing

bound[1]
past tense and past participle of bind; sure; obliged

bound[2]
(to) limit

bound[3]
going towards

boundary
dividing line
boundaries

bow[1]
weapon that shoots an arrow; knot with loops

bow[2]
gesture of respect made by lowering the head; to make a bow

bow[3]
forward end of ship

bowl[1]
round hollow container

bowl[2]
ball used in the game of bowls; (*cricket*) to throw the ball to the batsman

box[1]
container
boxes boxful

box[2]
to fight with gloved hands

boy
young human male
boyfriend boyhood boyish

bra
woman's undergarment supporting the breasts

brace
hand tool for drilling holes; clamping-device; pair; to support
bracing

bracket
support projecting from a wall; one of a pair of marks ( ) or []; to put between brackets
bracketed bracketing

brag
to boast
braggart bragged bragging

brain
part of the body inside the skull; centre of thought

brake
(to operate a) device for slowing down a vehicle
braking

branch
limb of a tree; subdivision; to divide
branches

brand
particular make of goods; (to mark with an) identifying mark

brass
alloy of copper and zinc

brave
showing courage; to face courageously
braver bravery bravest braving

breach
crack; breaking of a promise, rule, etc.; to make a breach
breaches

bread
food made from flour

breadth
distance from side to side

break
to (cause to) fall to pieces; gap or fracture; short rest or holiday
breakage broke broken

breakdown
mechanical failure; mental collapse

breakfast
first meal of the day

breast
female milk-producing gland; front part of the body between neck and stomach

breath
air drawn into and expelled from the lungs

breathe
to take air into and expel from the lungs
breathing

breed
to give birth to young; to raise livestock; to produce; particular type of animal
bred

breeze
gentle wind
breezily breeziness breezy

bribe
(to win over with a) gift offered to persuade or influence
bribable or *bribeable*
bribery bribing

brick
oblong building block made of clay

bride
woman at the time of her wedding
bridal

bridegroom
man at the time of his wedding

bridge[1]
structure over a river, etc.; to build a bridge over
bridging

bridge[2]
kind of card game

brief
short; official instructions; to give information to
briefs

bright
giving out much light; (informal) intelligent
brighten

brilliant
shining brightly; very clever
brilliance

brim
upper edge; rim of a hat; to fill
brimful brimmed brimming

bring
to carry; to cause
brought

broad
wide; full; general
broaden

broadcast
to transmit on radio or television; to scatter; radio or television transmission

brochure
pamphlet

broke
past tense of break

broken
past participle of break

brook
small stream

broom
long-handled brush; kind of shrub

brother
son of the same parents; male belonging to a group
brotherhood brother-in-law brothers-in-law brotherly

brought
past tense and past participle of bring

brow
forehead; top of a hill

brown
dark colour between orange and black

bruise
(to cause an) injury that discolours the skin
bruising

brush
(to clean with a) device containing bristles, hairs, etc.
brushes

bubble
thin spherical film of liquid inflated with air; (of a liquid) to have bubbles in it
bubblier bubbliest bubbling bubbly

bucket
open-topped container with handle for water, etc.
bucketful

buckle
(to fasten with a) clasp for belts or straps
buckling

bud
(to produce a) small swelling on a tree that develops into a flower, etc.
budded budding

budge
to move slightly
budging

budget
(to make an) estimate of the amount of money needed
budgetary budgeted budgeting

buffalo
kind of wild ox
buffaloes or *buffalos*

bug
kind of insect; germ;
(to install a) hidden listening device
bugged bugging

build
to make a structure
building built

bulb
round plant base; something shaped like this
bulbous

bulk
large amount; larger part
bulkier bulkiest bulkiness bulky

bull
adult male bovine animal

bullet
small round missile fired from a gun

bulletin
official statement of news

bully
person who uses his or her strength to make others feel afraid; to use one's strength to make others feel afraid
bullies bullied bullying

bump
(to strike with a) heavy impact
bumpier bumpiest bumpy

bun
small round cake; hair gathered into the shape of a bun

bunch
number of things growing or fastened together; to put or come together in a bunch
bunches

bundle
number of things loosely held together; to make a bundle
bundling

bungalow
one-storey house

buoy
floating marker for ships

buoyant
able to float; cheerful
buoyancy

burden
(to) load

bureau
writing-desk; office
bureaux or *bureaus*

bureaucracy
government by officials
bureaucracies bureaucrat bureaucratic bureaucratically

burger
savoury flat cake of minced meat

burglar
person who breaks into a building to steal
burglary burglaries burgle burgling

burial
burying

burn
to be on fire; to set fire to
burned or burnt

burrow
(to dig a) hole in the ground

burst
(to cause) to break open; rupture or outbreak

bury
to put in the ground and cover with earth
buried buries burying

bus
(to travel or transport by a) large passenger road vehicle
buses bused or *bussed busing* or *bussing*

bush
shrub; uncultivated land
bushes

business
trade; concern
businesses businesslike businessman businesswoman

bust[1]
sculpture of head, neck, and shoulders; woman's bosom

bust[2]
(informal) to break; broken; bankrupt

busy
(to keep) fully occupied
busied busier busies busiest busily busying busyness

but
however; except

butcher
retailer of meat; brutal killer
butchery

butter
(to spread with a) yellow fatty substance made from cream

butterfly
kind of insect with large wings
butterflies

button
knob of plastic, wood, etc., used as a fastener; to fasten with buttons
buttoned

buy
to obtain by payment of money
bought

by
near; beside; through the means or creation of

bye
(informal) goodbye

bypass
road that takes traffic around the centre of a busy town; medical operation to channel blood; to go around a busy area or blockage

Cc

cabbage
kind of leafy vegetable

cabin
ship or aircraft compartment; small simple dwelling

cabinet
piece of furniture; government executive and policy-making group

cable
length of wire; (to send a) telegram
cabling

cactus
kind of spiny plant
cacti or cactuses

caddy
small container for tea; (or caddie) person who carries a golfer's clubs
caddies

café
small or cheap restaurant

cafeteria
self-service restaurant

caffeine
alkaloid found in tea and coffee that acts as a stimulant

cage
(to put inside an) enclosure of wires or bars
caging

cake
baked mixture of flour, sugar, eggs, butter, etc.; to form a hard or thick mass
caking

calcium
white metallic element

calculate
to solve mathematically; to estimate
calculable calculating calculation calculator

calendar
display chart showing the days, weeks, and months of the year

calf[1]
of cattle, elephant, seal, etc.
calves

calf[2]
thick fleshy part of the leg between the knee and the ankle
calves

calibre (US **caliber**)
diameter of a cylinder, especially a gun barrel; ability
calibrate calibrating

call
(to give a) loud cry; to name; to summon; to make a short visit; to telephone

callous
insensitive; unfeeling

calm
(to make or become) still

calorie
unit of heat; unit measuring energy value of food
calories calorific

came
past tense of come

camel
humped, long-necked desert animal

camera
device for taking photographs
cameras

camouflage
(to conceal by) disguising so that something blends with its surroundings
camouflaging

camp
group of tents, huts, etc.; military quarters; to establish a camp
camping

campaign
series of planned activities or operations

campus
college or university grounds
campuses

can[1]
to be able or allowed to
cannot could

can[2]
(to preserve food in a) container
canned cannery canneries canning

canal
man-made water channel

cancel
to call off a meeting, etc.; to cross out
cancellation cancelled
(US *canceled*) *cancelling*
(US *canceling*)

candidate
person applying for a job, etc., or taking an examination
candidacy candidature

candle
wax stick with a wick that gives light when burned

cane
(to beat with the) long stem of certain plants
caning

cannon
kind of large heavy gun

canoe
(to travel by a) light narrow open boat
canoed canoeing canoeist

canon
member of clergy; church decree; standard, principle, or rule

canopy
overhanging cloth covering
canopies

can't
(informal) cannot

canteen
restaurant at a factory, school, etc.; box for a set of cutlery

canvas
heavy coarse cloth
canvases

canvass
to solicit votes or orders

cap
small soft hat; to cover
capped capping

capable
able; competent
capability capabilities capably

capacity
ability or power to contain or understand something; amount that can be contained
capacities

cape
sleeveless cloak; promontory

capital
main; punishable by death; place of government in a country; money to invest; large letter
capitalism capitalist

capitalize or capitalise
to write in capital letters; to provide with capital; to profit by
capitalization or *capitalisation*
capitalizing or *capitalising*

capsize
to overturn
capsizing

capsule
seed case; small soluble gelatin case for medicine; part of spacecraft for crew
capsular

captain
officer in charge of a ship; army or navy officer; leader
captaincy

captive
(held as) prisoner
captivity

capture
to take prisoner; to gain possession of
captor capturing

car
small road vehicle on wheels

caravan
(to travel in a) large enclosed vehicle that can be pulled by a car and is equipped for living in
caravanned caravanner caravanning

carbon
non-metallic element occurring in all organic compounds

card
small stiff piece of paper/plastic

cardboard
stiff thick paper for making boxes, etc.

cardiac
of the heart

care
(to give) close attention; (to feel) worry; to like
caring

career
one's life's work; to rush uncontrollably

careful
taking great care; cautious
carefully

careless
paying inadequate attention; negligent
carelessly

cargo
goods carried
cargoes or *cargos*

carpenter
person skilled in woodwork
carpentry

carpet
(to cover with a) heavy floor covering
carpeted carpeting

carriage
wheeled vehicle, esp. on a railway; act of conveying goods; body posture

carrier
person or thing that carries

carrot
kind of orange-red root vegetable

carry
to hold; to move or transport
carried carries carrying

cart
open vehicle

cartoon
humorous drawing

carve
to shape or cut
carver carving

case
(to put into a) container; suitcase; example or instance; legal action
casing

cash
(to exchange for) money

cashier
person responsible for receiving money in a shop; person who receives and pays out money in a bank

casserole
(food cooked in a) covered heatproof dish; to cook in a casserole
casseroling

cassette
small sealed container for magnetic tape or photographic film

cast
to throw; to vote; to shape an object; (to select the) performers in a play, etc.

castle
large fortified building

casual
happening by chance or accident; offhand; incidental

casualty
person injured or killed in an accident
casualties

cat
kind of small furry domestic animal; any feline animal

catalogue (US **catalog**)
(to) list
catalogued (US *cataloged*) *cataloguer* (US *cataloger*) *cataloguing* (US *cataloging*)

catastrophe
sudden great disaster
catastrophic

catch
to take hold of; act of this
catches caught

category
class or group
categories categorize or *categorise*

cater
to supply what is required, esp. food
caterer

caterpillar
wormlike larva of butterfly and moth

cathedral
principal church of a diocese

cattle
cows, bulls, etc.; bovine animals

caught
past tense and past participle of catch

cauliflower
kind of vegetable with a compact white flower-head

cause
that which produces an effect; to bring about; reason; charity
causal causality causing

caution
care; (to give) warning
cautionary cautious

cave
underground hollow; to collapse
caving

cease
to come to an end
ceasing

ceiling
upper surface of a room

celebrate
to observe a special occasion joyfully
celebrating celebration

celebrity
person
celebrities

celibate
(person who is) unmarried and not sexually active
celibacy

cell
small simple room; smallest part of a plant or animal
cellular

cellar
underground room, esp. for storage

cement
binding substance for building

cemetery
burial ground
cemeteries

censor
person with authority to remove objectionable parts from books, films, etc.
censorial censorious censorship

censure
to criticize strongly; to blame
censuring

census
official counting
censuses

cent
money unit of many countries

centenary
100th anniversary
centenaries

centimetre (US **centimeter**)
100th part of a metre

central
located in the centre; main
centralization or *centralisation* *centralize* or *centralise* *centralizing* or *centralising* *centrally*

centre (US **center**)
(to put at the) exact middle point
centring (US *centering*)

century
period of 100 years; 100 runs in cricket
centuries

cereal
grass plant producing an edible grain

ceremony
formal act or occasion
ceremonies ceremonial ceremonious

certain
sure; determined; some
certainly certainty certainties

certificate
official document

certify
to confirm or declare formally
certifiable certified certifies certifying

chain
length of metal links; unit of length, 22 yards; to confine

chair
seat with a back for one person; to preside over a meeting
chairman chairperson chairwoman

chalk
soft whitish limestone; piece of this used for writing

challenge
to call to justify oneself or compete; invitation to do this
challenging

chamber
hall or room

champagne
kind of white sparkling wine

champion
winner; someone who pleads a cause
championship

chance
(to take a) risk; fate or luck; opportunity
chancing chancy

chancellor
head of government in some European countries; high official; head of a university
chancellery chancellorship

change
to make or become different; to exchange money for smaller units or foreign currency; alteration or modification; money returned when one pays more than a thing costs
changeability changeable changing

channel
narrow stretch of water; (to direct along a) course or passage; band of frequencies
channelled (US *channeled*) *channelling* (US *channeling*)

chaos
utter confusion
chaotic chaotically

chap[1]
to become raw and cracked
chapped chapping

chap[2]
(informal) man

chapter
division of a book, etc.; (meeting of) cathedral clergy**character**
personal qualities; person in a play, story, etc.
characteristic characterization or *characterisation characterize* or *characterise characterizing* or *characterising*

charge
(to ask for as) payment; amount of electricity; (to make an) accusation
chargeable charging

charisma
great appeal and charm that inspires loyalty and enthusiasm
charismatic

charity
kindness; organization that helps the needy
charities charitable charitably

charm
quality of attraction; something thought to have magical powers
charming

chart
map; sheet or graph showing tables, etc.

charter
formal document granting rights; to hire an aircraft, boat, etc.

chase
to follow quickly; to hunt
chasing

chat
(to have a) friendly or informal talk
chatted chatting chatty

cheap
low in price; tawdry; worthless; *contemptible*

cheat
to behave dishonestly; person who cheats

check
to examine or inspect; to slow or stop

cheek
side of the face below the eye; insolence
cheekier cheekiest cheekily cheekiness cheeky

cheer
(to give) applause or shout of approval; (to give) encouragement; happy feeling
cheerful cheery

cheese
solid food made from milk
cheesy

chef
skilled cook

chemical
substance used in chemistry; relating to chemistry

chemist
someone trained in chemistry; dealer in medicines, etc.

chemistry
science dealing with the nature of substances and their reactions

cheque (US **check**)
written order instructing a bank to pay money

cherry
kind of small fleshy round fruit
cherries

chest
upper front part of the body; large sturdy case

chestnut
kind of tree; reddish-brown nut from such a tree

chew
to crush or grind food with the teeth
chewier chewiest chewy

chicken
young domestic fowl

chief
most important; main; head or leader
chiefs chiefly

child
young person; boy or girl
children childhood childish childlike

chill
(to make or become) cold
chillier chilliest chilly

chimney
vertical structure for carrying away smoke, etc.
chimneys

chin
front part of lower jaw

china
(articles made from) porcelain; crockery

chip
(to break off a) small piece of something; strip of fried potato; gambling token; wafer of silicon crystal
chipped chipping

chisel
tool for working or shaping wood
chiselled (US *chiseled*) *chiselling* (US *chiseling*)

chocolate
food prepared from cacao seeds
chocolatey

choice
choosing; selection; high-quality
choicer choicest

choir
organized group of singers

choke
to stop or hinder the breathing of; valve in petrol engine
choking

choose
to consider desirable
choosing chose chosen

chop
to cut or hit; thick cut of meat
*chopped chopping***chorus**
group of singers; repeated part of a song; to sing or utter together
choruses choral chorused chorusing

chose
past tense of choose
chosen past participle of *choose*

chronic
constantly recurring
chronically

chuck
(informal) to throw; to tap gently under the chin

church
place for public, esp. Christian, worship
churches

cigarette
thin tube of paper filled with shredded tobacco

cinema
theatre where films are shown
cinematic

circle
(to move in a) perfectly round plane figure
circling

circuit
(to make a) complete course; path of electric current
circuitous circuitry

circular
circle-shaped; leaflet, etc., for distribution
circularize or *circularise circularizing* or *circularising*

circulate
to move around a closed system; to spread widely; to talk to different people at a party, etc.
circulating circulation

circumstance
factor, condition, or detail
circumstantial

circus
travelling group of performing animals, acrobats, etc.
circuses

cite
to refer to; to give as an example
citation citing

citizen
inhabitant of a country, city, or town
citizenship

city
large and important town
cities

civic
relating to a town, city, or *citizens*

civil
relating to ordinary citizens; courteous
civility civilities civilly

civilian
(person) not belonging to the armed forces

civilize or **civilise**
to improve and educate; to refine
civilization or *civilisation* *civilizing* or *civilising*

clad
past tense of clothe

claim
(to demand as a) right
claimant

clamp
(to hold or fasten with a) mechanical gripping device

clap
to applaud by striking the hands together; sudden sharp sound
clapped clapper clapping

clash
(to make a) harsh noise; to come into conflict
clashes

class
(to put into a) group sharing a common characteristic; group of students taught together
classes

classic
typical; excellent; distinguished

classical
of ancient Greek and Roman cultures; (music) serious and in a traditional style

classify
to arrange in different groups
classifiable classification classified classifies classifying

classroom
room where a group of students are taught

clay
soft earthy material that hardens when baked

clean
(to make) free of dirt
cleaner

clear
(to make) bright; easy to see, hear, or understand; to empty
clearance

clerk
office-worker with general duties, esp. filing; (US) shop assistant
clerical

clever
intelligent; skilful

client
person seeking professional service or advice; customer
clientele

cliff
very steep high face of a rock

climate
normal general weather conditions of a place

climb
to go up

cling
to hold tightly (to)
clung

a b c d e f g h i j k l m n o p q r s t u v w x y z

clinic
centre for medical treatment and advice
clinical

clip
(to fasten with a) clasping device; to cut or trim
clipped clippers clipping

clock
device that measures and shows time
clockwork

close[1]
near; enclosed precinct
closer closest

close[2]
to shut; (to) finish

closet
small cupboard or room

cloth
woven fabric

clothe
to provide with clothes
clothed or *clad clothing*

clothes
articles of dress**cloud**
mass of water vapour; to become overcast with clouds; to make unclear
cloudier cloudiest cloudy

club
(to hit with a) heavy stick; group of people; society
clubbed clubbing

clue
helpful information to solve a problem; to inform
clued clueing or *cluing*

clumsy
awkward; unskilful; unwieldy
clumsier clumsiest clumsily clumsiness

clung
past tense and past participle of **cling**

cluster
number of things growing or occurring together

clutch
to seize tightly; coupling mechanism in motor vehicle
clutches

coach
railway carriage; long-distance bus; tutor or instructor; to instruct
coaches

coal
hard black mineral used as fuel

coalition
alliance of political parties

coarse
rough; crude or vulgar
coarser coarsest

coast
seashore; to move without using power
coastal

coat
outer garment with sleeves; covering of animal; layer of paint, etc.

cock
male domestic fowl; valve or tap; to set upright or tilt; to set (a gun) ready for firing

cocoa
(drink made from) powdered cocoa beans

cod
kind of large sea-fish

code
secret system of letters or symbols; set of principles or rules

coffee
(kind of drink made from the roasted and ground seeds of a) tropical shrub

cohabit
to live together as husband and wife
cohabitant cohabitation

coherent
well-planned; consistent; intelligible
cohere coherence

coil
(to wind in a) spiral

coin
piece of metal money; to create
coinage

coincide
to happen at the same time; to agree
coincidence coincidental coinciding

cold
having a low temperature; passive or indifferent; viral infection marked by sneezing, etc.

collaborate
to work in partnership
collaborating collaboration collaborator

collapse
to break or give way; to cave in; act of doing this
collapsible collapsing

collar
part of a garment fitting round the neck

colleague
fellow worker

collect
to bring or come together; to fetch
collectable or *collectible collector*

collection
collecting; group of things that have been collected

collective
involving all the members of a group

college
institution of higher education
collegiate

collide
to come together forcibly
colliding collision

colony
settlement or settlers in a new territory
colonies colonial colonist colonization or *colonisation colonize* or *colonise colonizing* or *colonising*

colossal
huge; gigantic

colour (US **color**)
visual sensation produced by light rays; paint; badge or flag
colourful (US *colorful*)

column
upright pillar; vertical printed section
columnist

comb
toothed device for cleaning and arranging hair; crest of a fowl

combat
(to) fight or struggle
combatant combated combating combative

combine
to join together; union
combination combining

come
to move towards the speaker
came coming

comedy
light humorous play
comedies comedian comedienne

comfort
contentment; (to give) encouragement

comfortable
pleasant and giving comfort or ease; feeling no pain, anxiety, etc.
comfortably

comic
intended to amuse; comedian; children's magazine
comical comically

command
(to give an) authoritative direction or order
commandant commander commandment

commemorate
to honour the memory of
commemorating commemoration commemorative

comment
(to make a) remark or observation
commentator

commentary
set of comments or description of something
commentaries

commerce
business; trade

commercial
relating to business or trade; television or radio advertisement
commercialization or *commercialisation commercialize* or *commercialise commercializing* or *commercialising commercially*

commission
task; official group entrusted with authority, esp. by government; rank of officer in the armed forces; percentage paid to an agent; to grant authority to

commit
to entrust; to perform
commitment committed committing

committee
group of people appointed to carry out a service or function

commodity
article of commerce
commodities

common
general; ordinary; open public land

communicate
to convey; to transmit news
communicable communicating communication communicative

communism
social system in which the means of production are owned and controlled by the state
communist

community
group of people living in one area
communities

companion
someone accompanying another person
companionable companionship

company
business organization; time spent with someone
companies

compare
to find out similarities and differences between
comparable comparative comparing comparison

compartment
divided section, esp. of an enclosed space
compartmentalize or *compartmentalise*

compass
instrument that shows magnetic north; instrument for drawing circles

compel
to force
compelled compelling

compensate
to make amends for loss or damage
compensating compensation

compete
to take part in a contest; to try to do better than
competing

competent
capable; qualified
competence

competition
contest involving rivalry
competitive competitor

complain
to express discontent
complaint

complement
something that completes; to make complete
complementary

complete
whole; thorough; finished; total; to make complete
completely completing completion

complex
difficult; made up of several different parts; set of feelings that affect behaviour
complexes complexity complexities

complexion
colouring and appearance of the facial skin

complicate
to make difficult to understand
complicated complicating complication

compliment
expression of admiration; to express admiration
complimentary

comply
to do as a person asks
compliance compliant complied complies complying

compose
to create; to make up; to calm
composing composition compositor composure

compound
(something) made up of two or more parts; enclosed area; to combine to make a whole

comprehend
to understand; to include
comprehensibility comprehensible comprehensibly comprehension

comprehensive
including everything; type of secondary school

compromise
(to reach a) settlement of a dispute by concessions made on both sides; to expose to disrepute
compromising

compulsory
required by laws, rules, etc.
compulsion compulsorily

computer
electronic calculating machine that can store and process information
compute computing

concede
to admit; to yield
conceding

conceit
exaggerated opinion of oneself
conceited

conceive
to imagine; to become pregnant
conceivable conceivably conceiving conception

concentrate
to focus the mind, one's efforts, etc., (on); to make pure by removing certain parts
concentrating concentration

concept
general idea; thought
conception conceptual

concern
to relate to; (to) worry; business

concerning
relating to; about

concert
musical performance; to plan with others

concession
something conceded, such as a demand or right
concessionaire concessionary concessive

conclude
to end; to decide
concluding conclusion conclusive

concrete
(to set in a) building material; real; specific
concreting concretion

condemn
to disapprove of strongly; to pronounce a sentence on
condemnation

condition
a state or circumstance; necessary requirement; to influence
conditional

conduct
behaviour; to guide or direct
conductor

confer
to bestow; to discuss
conferred conferring

conference
formal discussion

confess
to admit one's faults; to declare
confesses confession confessional confessor

confidence
trust; self-assurance
confident

confidential
private or secret
confidentiality confidentially

confine
to restrict
confinement confining

confirm
to prove, state, etc., to be true or valid
confirmation

conflict
(to) fight; (to) clash

confront
to bring or come face to face with
confrontation

confuse
to muddle in the mind; to blur
confusing confusion

congratulate
to speak to someone with praise and admiration for a success or happy event
congratulating congratulation congratulations congratulatory

congress
meeting or conference
congresses congressional

conjunction
union; (grammar) word linking other words or phrases

conjure
to perform magic tricks; to imagine or cause to appear
conjuring conjuror or *conjurer*

connect
to join or be joined
connection or *connexion connector*

conquer
to overcome or defeat
conqueror conquest

conscience
sense of right and wrong

conscientious
meticulous; hard-working

conscious
fully awake; aware
consciousness

consensus
general agreement

consequence
result; significance or importance
consequent consequently

conservation
keeping from change, decay, etc.
conserve conserving

consider
to think carefully about
considerate consideration considering

considerable
large; significant
considerably

consist
to be composed (of)

consistent
conforming with previous behaviour, practice, etc.
consistently

consonant
speech sound or letter of the alphabet that is not a vowel

constant
unchanging; happening continually; loyal
constancy

constituency
body of voters who elect an MP
constituencies

constitute
to form; to appoint
constituting constitutive

constitution
set of principles by which a country, etc., is run; structure or condition
constitutional

constrain
to force
constraint

construct
to build
construction constructor

constructive
suggesting improvement; positive

consult
to ask advice from
consultant consultation consultative

consume
to eat or drink; to use up
consumable consumer consumerism consuming

consumption
consuming; tuberculosis of the lungs
consumptive

contact
(to) touch; to communicate with

contain
to hold or include

container
something in which one keeps things; large box of standard size for the transport of goods
containerization or *containerisation* *containerize* or *containerise*

contemporary
modern; (person) living at the same time
contemporaries contemporaneous

contempt
despising; scorn
contemptible contemptuous

content[1]
happy; satisfied; to satisfy
contented contentment

content[2]
something that is contained; substance, not form

contest
(to) fight or struggle; test of skill, etc.
contestant

context
particular setting or conditions of words or events
contextual

continent
one of the earth's large land masses
continental

continual
regularly repeated
continually

continue
to go on; to carry on doing
continuation continuing *continuity*

continuous
in an uninterrupted or unbroken series or pattern; not ceasing
continuously

contract
(to undertake by a) formal agreement; to reduce in size; to catch an infection
contraction contractor contractual

contradict
to state the opposite; to declare to be untrue
contradiction contradictory

contrary
(something) opposite or opposed; stubborn
contraries contrarily contrariness

contrast
to distinguish by showing different features; such *differences*

contribute
to give with others; to supply
contributing contribution contributor

control
(to exercise) power, authority, or direction; to restrain
controllable controlled controller controlling

controversy
matter for dispute
controversies controversial

convenient
suitable; easy to use
convenience

a b c d e f g h i j k l m n o p q r s t u v w x y z

convention
generally accepted principle; large formal meeting
conventional conventionality

conversation
talk between two or more people
conversational

convert
to change or transform
conversion converter or *convertor convertibility convertible*

convey
to carry, transport, or *communicate*

convict
to pronounce guilty; person found guilty and sentenced to imprisonment conviction convicting; strongly held belief

convince
to make someone believe
convincing

cook
to prepare food by heating; person who does this
cooker cookery

cool
moderately cold; to calm
coolly

cooperate
to work together for a common purpose
cooperating cooperation cooperative

coordinate
to combine or harmonize; number specifying a location; one of a set of matching clothes
coordinating coordination coordinator

cope
to deal successfully (with)
coping

copper
reddish-brown metallic element

copy
(to make an) imitation or exact reproduction
copies copied copier copying

cord
string or rope made of twisted strands; something resembling this, e.g., a part of the body or an electrical wire

core
central part, esp. of an apple; to remove the core from
corer coring

corn
kind of cereal plant; (US) maize; hard thick skin area, esp. on the toe

corner
angle or point where two lines or surfaces meet; to monopolize

corporate
shared; joint

corporation
local authority of a town or city; large business organization

corpse
dead body

correct
(to make) right, accurate, or approved
correction

correspond
to agree (with); to communicate (with) by letter
correspondence correspondent

corridor
passage

corroborate
to support or confirm
corroborating corroboration corroborative

corrupt
(to make) dishonest or depraved
corruptible corruption

cost
(to) price

costly
expensive
costlier costliest costliness

cottage
small simple house

cotton
soft fibrous substance made from the seeds of the cotton plant

cough
to expel air from the lungs with a short sharp sound

could
past tense of can1
couldn't

council
elected group or committee
councillor (US *councilor*)

counsel
(to give) advice; barristers
counselled (US *counseled*) *counselling* (US *counseling*) *counsellor* (US *counselor*)

count
to check, reckon, or add up with numbers

counter[1]
raised level surface over which business is transacted; small disc used in games

counter[2]
to oppose; (in a direction that is) opposite

country
territory of a nation; land with open fields or woods
countries countryside

county
administrative division of a country
counties

couple
(to) pair; to link
coupling

coupon
form of ticket entitling the holder to obtain an article or service

courage
bravery
courageous

course
direction; procedure; series of lessons, lectures, etc.

court
enclosed area for games; sovereign and retinue; legal tribunal; to seek favour from; to woo

courtesy
politeness; respect; favour
courtesies courteous

cousin
child of one's uncle or aunt

cover
to spread over, esp. as a protection; to extend over; something that covers
coverage covering

cow
female of certain animals, esp. domesticated cattle

coward
person without courage or who shrinks from danger
cowardice cowardliness cowardly

crack
(to) break; (to make a) sudden sharp noise

cradle
(to support as in a) baby's bed on rockers
cradling

craft
activity needing skill; skill or cunning; vessel, aircraft, etc.
craftier craftiest crafty

crane
kind of large wading bird; device for lifting and moving heavy objects; to stretch out the neck
craning

crash
(to make or hit with a) sudden noisy smashing sound
crashes

crawl
to move slowly with the body close to the ground; swimming stroke; to act in a servile way

crayon
(to draw or colour with a) stick of coloured wax, etc.

crazy
insane; (of paving) made up of irregular pieces
crazier craziest crazily craziness

creak
(to make a) harsh squeaking or grating noise

cream
(to remove the) fatty part of milk

crease
mark or line made by pressing or folding; to make such a mark
creasing

create
to cause to exist
creating creation creative creativity creator

creature
living being, esp. an animal

credible
believable; trustworthy
credibility credibly

credit
money in a bank account; money lent by a bank; approval or acknowledgement; (to) trust
creditable creditor

creep
to move slowly with the body close to the ground
crept

crew
people working on a ship or aircraft; group working together

cricket
outdoor team-game played with bats and ball

cried
past tense and past participle of cry

crime
offence prohibited and punishable by law

criminal
person who is guilty of a crime; of crime
criminality

crisis
time of extreme trouble or danger; crucial point
crises

crisp
brittle and dry; thin slice of fried potato

criterion
standard of judgement or decision
criteria

critic
person who judges, evaluates, or finds fault

critical
fault-finding; of or at a crisis; evaluating

criticize or **criticise**
to find fault with; to analyse
criticism criticizing or *criticising*

crocodile
kind of tropical reptile with massive jaws

crop
product that is grown and harvested; kind of whip; to cut short; to gather a crop
cropped cropping

cross
structure or symbol of vertical post with beam across; X-shaped mark; to move across; angry
crosses

crouch
to bend low to the ground

crowd
(to gather in a) large number of people

crown
ornamental head-dress of a monarch; to place a crown on the head of; (to form the) top part of

crucial
decisive
crucially

crude
unrefined; rough; coarse
cruder crudest crudity

cruel
taking pleasure in causing pain
crueller (US *crueler*) *cruellest* (US *cruelest*) *cruelly cruelty cruelties*

crush
to destroy by pressing down; large number of people in a restricted space
crushes

crust
hard outer covering

cry
(to) shout; to weep
cries cried crying

crystal
transparent kind of quartz; high-quality glass; regular-shaped piece of substance
crystalline crystallize or crystallise

cue[1]
signal for an actor to speak; to give a cue to
cued cuing

cue[2]
long tapering rod used in billiards or snooker

cultivate
to prepare land for crops; to grow
cultivating cultivation cultivator

culture
traditions, customs, etc., of a people; appreciation of the arts; cultivation
cultural

cup
drinking bowl with a handle; to form into a cup shape
cupped cupping

cupboard
piece of furniture or recessed area of a room

cure
to restore to health; to preserve food; restoration to health
curability curable curative curing

curiosity
eagerness to learn; unusual thing
curiosities

curious
eager to learn; unusual

curl
(to twist into a) spiral or wave
curlier curliest curly

currency
money; general acceptance and use
currencies

current
stream or flow of water, air, or electricity; contemporary; in general use

curriculum
course of study
curricula or curriculums

curry
food flavoured with hot-tasting spices, etc.
curries

curse
to call evil on; (to utter) profane swearing language
cursing

curtain
fabric hung as a screen, esp. at a window

curve
(to form into a) continuously bending line
curvaceous curvature curving

cushion
bag made of fabric and filled with feathers, etc.; to reduce the impact of

custom
tradition; patronage

customary
traditional; usual
customarily

customer
buyer

customs
duty on imports or exports; government agency or area of a port for collection of such duties

cut
(to make a) slit or opening; to divide; wound; to shorten
cutter cutting

cycle
recurring series of events; complete set; bicycle or motor cycle; to ride a bicycle
cyclic cyclical cycling cyclist

cylinder
tube-shaped object
cylindrical

Dd

dad
(informal) father
daddy daddies

daily
(happening) every day; daily newspaper
dailies

dainty
small and delicate; delicacy
dainties daintier daintiest daintily daintiness

dairy
place where milk, butter, etc., are kept or sold
dairies

dam
(to restrict by a) barrier across a river, etc.
dammed damming

damage
(to cause) harm, loss, or injury
damageable damaging

damn
to condemn as bad; to condemn to the punishment of hell; to swear
damnable damned damnedest or damndest

damp
(to make) slightly wet
dampen

dance
to move the body in time to music
dancer dancing

danger
risk; peril
dangerous

dare
to be brave enough; to challenge
daren't daring

dark
with little or no light
darken darkly darkness

darling
dearly loved (person)

dash
to move quickly; punctuation mark –
dashes

data
facts, observations, or information

date[1]
(to mark the) day, month, and year of an event
dating

date[2]
edible fruit of tall palm

daughter
female child of parents
daughter-in-law daughters-in-law

dawn
daybreak; to begin to appear

day
period of 24 hours; time of light

daylight
light from the sun that makes things visible in daytime

daytime
the period of the day when it is light

dead
no longer alive; complete
deaden

deadline
time limit

deadly
capable of causing death; (informal) boring
deadlier deadliest deadliness

deaf
unable to hear
deafen

deal
to distribute; to be concerned (with); to trade (in) business transaction; large quantity
dealer dealings dealt

dear
well-loved; precious; expensive

death
ending of life

debate
(to take part in a) formal discussion
debatable debater debating

debt
something owed
debtor

début
or debut first public appearance

decade
period of 10 years

decay
(to) rot

deceive
to mislead deliberately
deceit deceitful deceiver deceiving

December
12th month of the year

decent
proper; respectable
decency

deception
act of deceiving
deceptive

decide
to make up one's mind; to settle
decidedly deciding

decision
act of deciding; conclusion
decisive

deck
floor of a ship or bus

declare
to make known or announce; to state emphatically
declaration declaring

decline
to refuse; to lose power, strength, etc.; (*grammar*) to give the case endings of a noun, etc.
declining

decorate
to ornament; to paint, wallpaper, etc.
decorating decoration decorative decorator

decrease
to lessen or diminish
decreasing

dedicate
to consecrate; to devote (to)
dedicating dedication

deduct
to take away or subtract
deduction

deed
act or achievement; legal *document*

deep
extending far down
deepen

deer
kind of 4-footed animal, the male of which usually has branched horns

defeat
to overcome; loss of a fight, contest, etc.
defeatism defeatist

defect
flaw or imperfection; to desert one's country, cause, etc.
defection defective defector

defence
(US defense) protection or resistance against attack

defend
to protect against attack
defensible defensive

defendant
person who is on trial

deficit
amount by which a sum of money is less than required or expected

define
to state the meaning of
defining definition

definite
clear; certain; decided
definitely definitive decisive; authoritative and comprehensive

defy
to disobey openly
defiance defied defies defying

degree
unit of measurement of temperature or angles; stage in scale; academic qualification

delay
to put off to a later time

delegate
someone representing and acting on behalf of others; to appoint as a delegate; to entrust (a task) to a subordinate
delegation

deliberate
intentional; to consider carefully
deliberately deliberating deliberation

delicate
fine or subtle; fragile; sensitive
delicacy delicately

delicious
pleasant to the senses, esp. taste

delight
great pleasure; to please greatly
delighted delightful

deliver
to hand over; to take; to set free; to help to bring to birth
deliverance delivery deliveries

demand
to ask for urgently; consumers' willingness and ability to buy something

demanding
difficult; requiring a lot of effort

demeanour (US **demeanor**)
behaviour

democracy
government by the people
democracies democrat democratic

demolish
to pull down or destroy
demolishes demolition

demonstrate
to show or explain clearly with evidence; to protest publicly
demonstrable demonstrating demonstration demonstrative demonstrator

denial
declaration that something is untrue

dense
thick; complicated; (informal) stupid
density

dentist
someone qualified in the care of teeth
dentistry

deny
to declare to be untrue
deniable denied denies denying

deodorant
substance that removes or masks unwanted smells

depart
to leave; to go away

department
specialized division
departmental

departure
act of going away

depend
to rely (on); to trust
dependable dependence

dependant (US **dependent**)
person who relies on another for esp. financial support
dependent relying on; subject to

depict
to show by a drawing or picture
depiction

deposit
to put or set down, esp. for safekeeping; money paid in part payment; money paid into a bank; layer
deposition depositor

depot
storehouse; place where buses or railway engines are maintained

depress
to discourage; to push down
depressant depressed depresses depression depressive

deprive
to take away from
deprivation depriving

depth
distance downwards; deepness

deputy
person chosen to act on behalf of another
deputies depute deputize or *deputise*

descend
to move downwards
descent

descendant
person or animal who is a later member of the same family

describe
to give an account or representation of in words
describing description descriptive

desert[1]
area of dry infertile land

desert[2]
to abandon

deserve
to be worthy of
deserving

design
(to draw a) plan or sketch
designer

designate
appointed to office but not yet taking office; to indicate, specify, or name
designating designation

desirable
attractive
desirability desirably

desire
to wish or long for; longing
desiring

desk
piece of furniture used for reading and writing

despair
to lose all hope; loss of all hope
despairingly

despatch *see* **dispatch**

desperate
despairing
desperation

despite
in spite of

dessert
sweet course at a meal

destroy
to ruin or demolish; to put an end to
destruction destructive

detach
to separate without damage
detached detaches detachment

detail
individual item or part
detailed

detect
to discover; to find someone committing an offence
detectable or *detectible detection detector*

detective
police officer employed to solve crimes

determination
firmness of purpose; *determining*

determine
to decide; to be firm
determinable determined

deterrent
(something) that discourages someone from attempting something
deterrence

devastate
to lay waste; to ravage; to distress greatly
devastated devastating devastation

develop
to (cause to) grow or mature; to appear or acquire gradually; to produce a photograph chemically
developed developer developing development developmental

device
machine or tool; scheme

devil
(supreme) evil spirit; to season food highly
devilish devilled (US *deviled*) *devilling* (US *deviling*) *devilment devilry*

devise
to work out or plan in the mind
devising

devote
to apply or give (oneself) to
devotee devoting devotion

diagnosis
identification of diseases by examining symptoms
diagnoses diagnose diagnosing diagnostic

diagram
drawn plan or design
diagrammatic

dial
numbered disc on a telephone, face of a clock, etc.; to operate a telephone dial
dialled dialling

dialogue (US **dialog**)
conversation between 2 people

diameter
line across the centre of a circle or sphere
diametric diametrical diametrically

diamond
very hard precious stone; 4-sided figure

diarrhoea (US **diarrhea**)
abnormally frequent and liquid bowel movements

diary
personal record of daily events, appointments, etc.
diaries diarist

dictate
to say aloud for a person to write down or for a machine to record; to give orders authoritatively
dictating dictation dictator dictatorial

dictionary
book consisting of an alphabetical list of words and their meanings
dictionaries

did
past tense of **do**

didn't
(informal) did not

die
to stop living
dying

diet
(to keep to a) special range of foods
dietary dietetics dietician

differ
to be unlike; to disagree

different
unlike or not the same as
difference

differentiate
to show the difference;
to distinguish
differentiating differentiation

difficult
not easy; requiring skill
or effort
difficulty difficulties

dig
to break up or take away earth
digger digging dug

digest
to break down food into easily
absorbed substances; to absorb
mentally; summary
digestible digestion digestive

digital
concerning information in the form of
electronic signals

dignity
being worthy of respect
dignify dignified dignifying

dimension
measurement in a particular direction
dimensional

diminish
to reduce in size, value, or quantity
diminishes diminution

dinner
main meal of the day

dinosaur
large extinct reptile

dip
to plunge or drop; to slope
downwards; creamy mixture
dipped dipper dipping

diplomacy
conduct of international relations;
tact
diplomat diplomatic diplomatically

direct
straightforward; to point out the way;
to order
directive

direction
way to a place; supervising;
instruction
directional

director
board-member of a firm; supervisor
directorate directorship

directory
book listing names, addresses, and
telephone numbers of people or
businesses in an area
directories

dirt
unclean substance

dirty
(to make) unclean
dirtied dirtier dirties dirtiest dirtily dirtiness dirtying

disable
to deprive of an ability
disabled disability disabilities disabling

disadvantage
unfavourable circumstance, thing, etc.; to handicap
disadvantaged disadvantageous

disagree
to have a different point of view; to have unpleasant effects on
disagreeable disagreed disagreeing disagreement

disappear
to stop being visible
disappearance

disappoint
to fail to come up to the expectations of
disappointed disappointment

disapprove
to consider wrong; to reject
disapproval disapproving

disaster
event causing great destruction or misfortune
disastrous

disc (US **disk**)
thin flat circular object; gramophone record

discharge
to dismiss or release; to emit; to fulfil

discipline
(to train to produce) self-control and obedience
disciplinarian disciplinary disciplining

discontent
dissatisfaction
discontented

discount
reduction in price; to consider unimportant

discover
to find for the first time; to find out
discovery discoveries

discreet
cautious and tactful; modest

discretion
cautious and sensitive behaviour; right to make decisions
discretionary

discriminate
to treat as different, esp. because of prejudice; to distinguish
discriminating discrimination

discuss
to have a conversation about
discusses discussion

disease
illness
diseased

disguise
to change the appearance of in order to hide identity; something that does this
disguising

disgust
(to cause) great loathing

dish
(to serve in a) shallow open vessel
dishes

dislike
(to consider with) disapproval

dismiss
to discharge from employment, etc.; to send away
dismissal dismisses dismissive

disorder
confusion; to disturb
disorderliness disorderly

dispatch or **despatch**
to send away; message
dispatches or *despatches*

dispense
to give out; to manage without
dispensable dispensary dispensaries dispensation dispenser dispensing

disperse
to scatter
dispersing

display
(to) show; to present

displease
to annoy or upset
displeasing displeasure

dispose
to get rid (of); to deal with; to place in order
disposable disposal disposing disposition

dispute
to quarrel or argue; quarrel or argument
disputable disputation disputing

disrupt
to throw into a disorganized state; to break up
disruption disruptive

dissatisfy
to fail to fulfil someone's hopes or expectations
dissatisfaction dissatisfied dissatisfies dissatisfying

dissolve
to make or become liquid by soaking; to end officially
dissolution dissolving

distance
space between two points; to keep at a distance
distancing

distant
remote

distinct
clear; noticeable

distinction
difference; noble quality; specially high mark in an examination

distinctive
characteristic

distinguish
to show the difference between; to bring honour to
distinguishable distinguishes

distinguished
noble; famous

distress
(to cause) anguish or suffering
distresses distressing

distribute
to share out; to circulate
distributing distribution distributive distributor

district
area of land, esp. for administrative purposes

disturb
to interrupt; to destroy the quietness or order of
disturbance

dive
to plunge head first into water
dived (US *dove*) *diving*

divide
to separate; to distribute
dividing divisibility divisible divisive divisor

dividend
number to be divided; money payable to shareholders

division
dividing; divided part; category
divisional

divorce
legal ending of a marriage; to end a marriage by divorce
divorcee divorcing

do
to carry out; to produce; function or gathering
dos did doable does doing done

doctor
qualified medical practitioner; person with higher academic degree; to treat or modify; to castrate
doctorate

document
written, esp. official, statement providing evidence or information
documentary documentation

doesn't
(*informal*) does not

dog
domesticated canine animal; to follow closely and persistently
dogged dogging doggy doggies

doll
small toy model of a human; to dress (up)
dolly dollies

dollar
money unit of USA, Canada, Australia, etc.

domestic
of the home or family
domestically domesticate domesticating domesticity

dominate
to control or influence; to overlook
dominance dominant dominating domination

donate
to give to charity
donating donation donor

done
past participle of do

donkey
ass; stubborn person
donkeys

don't
(informal) do not

door
barrier closing and opening the entrance to a house or room

doorway
the space opened and closed by a door

dose
(to give a) measured quantity of medicine
dosage dosing

dot
(to make a) small round mark
dotted dotting

double
(to make) twice the amount
doubling doubly

doubt
(to have) disbelief and uncertainty
doubtful doubtfully doubtless

down
from a higher to a lower position; in a lower position

downstairs
on or to a lower floor in a building

downwards
from a higher to a lower position
downward

dozen
12

draft
(to make a) rough sketch; order to pay money; (US) conscription or to conscript
draftee

drag
to pull slowly and with difficulty; to trail along the ground
dragged dragging

drain
(to remove liquid through a) pipe, channel, etc.
drainage

drama
theatrical play; highly emotional event
dramatic dramatically dramatist

drank
past tense of **drink**

draught (US **draft**)
flow of air; depth of water; pulling a load; drawing beer, etc., from a barrel

draw
to pull; to take out; to make a picture; to finish equal
drawn drew

drawer
person or thing that draws; compartment that slides in and out of a piece of furniture

dreadful
very disagreeable or bad
dreadfully

dream
to have a series of images, thoughts, etc., during sleep
dreamed or *dreamt dreamy*

dress
to put on clothes; woman's garment; to apply bandages to a wound
dresses

drew
past tense of **draw**

dried
past tense and past participle of **dry**

drier
comparative of **dry**; (or **dryer**) machine for drying

drift
to be carried along by a current; something piled up; gist or general meaning

drill
(to use a) machine or tool for boring holes; (to instruct with) military training

drink
(to swallow) liquid
drank drunk

drip
(to allow) to fall in drops
dripped dripping

drive
to operate a vehicle; to cause to move forcefully; journey; road
driven driver drove

drop
small quantity of liquid; (to allow) to fall
dropped dropper dropping

drown
to die or kill by submerging in water

drug
substance used in treating a disease; substance that causes addiction; to use a drug
drugged drugging druggist

drum
(to play a) musical instrument with a skin stretched over a hollow cylinder
drummed drummer drumming

drunk
past participle of **drink**; intoxicated with alcohol
drunkard drunken drunkenly drunkenness

dry
(to make or become) free from moisture
dried drier or *dryer dries driest drily* or *dryly drying*

duck[1]
kind of swimming-bird; batsman's score of nil in cricket

duck[2]
to lower the head or body quickly

due
payable; owing; expected; (something) deserved
duly

dug
past tense and past participle of **dig**

dull
(to make) not bright or not sharp; slow or boring
dully

duly
in a proper manner

dumb
unable to speak; (*informal*) stupid

dump
to put down carelessly; to throw away; place for depositing rubbish

durable
able to be used or lasting for a long time
durability durably

during
throughout; at a point of time within

dust
(to wipe or brush away) fine particles of earth or dirt
dustier dustiest dusty

duty
tax; obligation
duties dutiable dutiful

dye
(to change the colour of by applying) liquid colouring substance
dyes dyed dyeing dyer

dying
present participle of **die**

dynamic
active and energetic; of a motive force
dynamically dynamism

Ee

each
every (one)

eager
keen; enthusiastic

ear
organ of hearing

early
at or near the start of a time; before the usual time
earlier earliest earliness

earn
to receive money in return for work
earnings

earnest
serious; determined; money given to seal a bargain; pledge

earth
planet on which we live; land; not sea or air; soil; to connect an electrical device to earth
earthenware earthly earthquake earthy

ease
(to give) freedom or relief from pain
easing

east
one of the 4 compass points; direction of sunrise
easterly eastern easterner eastward eastwards

easy
not difficult
easier easiest easily easiness

eat
to take into the mouth and swallow
ate eaten eating

echo
(to resound as a) reflection of sound waves
echoes echoed echoing

ecology
study of the relationship between living things and their environment
ecological ecologist

economic
of a country's economy; profitable
economically

economical
not needing a lot of money; prudent

economy
system of making goods and using resources; thriftiness; action intended to save money
economies economics economist economize or *economise*

ecstasy
intense joy
ecstasies ecstatic ecstatically

edge
border; limit; side; to move gradually
edginess edging edgy

edit
to prepare for publication; to be in charge of a newspaper, etc.; to arrange film, tape, etc., for broadcasting
edition editor editorial

educate
to teach and train; to develop the character, mind, etc., of
educating education educational educator

effect
something produced by a cause

effective
producing the desired result

effectively
so as to produce the desired result; actually or to all intents and purposes

efficient
working well; producing the desired effect with the least waste
efficiency

effort
physical or mental exertion; attempt

egg
reproductive body produced by birds, animals, etc.

ego
person's inner self; self-esteem
egocentric egocentricity egoism egoist egotism egotist

eight
number 8
eighth

eighteen
number 18
eighteenth

eighty
number 80
eighties eightieth

either
1 or the other (of 2); likewise

elaborate
complicated; developed carefully; to describe in detail
elaborating elaboration

elastic
springy; flexible rubber fabric
elastically elasticate elasticity

elbow
joint where the arm bends

elder[1]
(person who is) older; church leader
eldest

elder[2]
kind of bush with berries
elderberry

elderly
quite old

elect
to choose by vote; chosen, but not yet in office
election electioneer elective elector electoral electorate

electric
of, worked by, or producing *electricity*
electrical electrically electrician

electricity
power that gives heat and light and drives machines

electronic
operated by small components such as microchips and transistors
electronically

element
part that makes up a whole; basic chemical substance
elemental

elementary
very easy; basic

elephant
large mammal with trunk and long tusks

eleven
number 11
eleventh

eliminate
to remove or reject completely
eliminating elimination

else
besides; apart from; otherwise

elsewhere
in or to another place than this

email or **e-mail**
electronic mail

embargo
(to place a) temporary ban on trade
embargoes embargoed embargoing

embarrass
to make self-conscious or awkward
embarrassed embarrasses embarrassing embarrassment

embed
to place or fix firmly in
embedded embedding

embody
to incorporate; to give definite form to
embodied embodies embodiment embodying

embrace
to clasp in one's arms; to use
embracing

emerge
to come out; to come into view
emergence emergent emerging

emergency
serious unexpected event demanding immediate action
emergencies

emotion
strong feeling of joy, sorrow, etc.

emotional
of the emotions

emphasis
special importance; stress
emphases emphatic emphatically

emphasize or **emphasise**
to put emphasis on
emphasizing or *emphasising*

empire
group of countries ruled by one supreme authority
emperor empress imperial

employ
to provide with a paid job; (formal) to use
employment

employee
person employed

employer
person or firm that employs people

empty
containing nothing; to make or become empty; something that is empty
empties emptied emptier emptiest emptiness emptying

enable
to make possible or practical
enabling

enclose
to shut in; to surround; to insert
enclosing enclosure

encounter
to come upon; to meet; meeting

encourage
to inspire with courage and confidence
encouragement encouraging

encyclopedia or **encyclopaedia**
book containing information on a wide range of subjects
encyclopedic or *encyclopaedic*

end
(to come or bring to the) final or extreme limit or point

ending
last or concluding part

endless
never-ending

enemy
person or group that is hostile to another
enemies enmity

energetic
active and full of energy
energetically

energy
power for activity or work
energies energize or *energise*

engage
to gain the service of; to hold the attention of
engaging

engaged
pledged to be married
engagement

engine
machine that converts energy into work or power

engineer
person skilled in the design, construction, and use of machines and structures
engineering

enhance
to heighten an attractive quality of
enhancing

enjoy
to receive pleasure from
enjoyable enjoyably enjoyment

enlarge
to make or become larger
enlargement enlarger enlarging

enormous
unusually great in size, extent, or degree
enormity

enough
sufficient

enquire
to ask
enquirer enquiring enquiry enquiries

ensure (US **insure**)
to make certain or sure
ensuring (US *insuring*)

enter
to go or come into

enterprise
project or undertaking; initiative
enterprising

entertain
to amuse; to show hospitality to

enthral (US **enthrall**)
to hold the complete attention of
enthralled enthralling

enthusiasm
great liking and interest
enthusiast enthusiastic enthusiastically

entire
complete; total
entirely entirety

entitle
to give the right to
entitlement entitling

entrance[1]
act of entering; way in

entrance[2]
to fill with intense delight; to enchant
entrancing

entrepreneur
controller of a business enterprise
entrepreneurial

entry
entrance
entries

envelop
to wrap or cover; to obscure or hide
envelopment

envelope
folded paper cover for letter

environment
surroundings; circumstances or external conditions
environmental environmentalist

envy
(to have a) feeling of grudging discontent at the possessions or qualities of another
enviable envied envies envious envying

equal
(to have the) same amount, quality, value, etc.
equality equalled (US *equaled*) *equalling* (US *equaling*) *equally*

equalize or **equalise**
to make equal
equalization or *equalisation equalizer* or *equaliser equalizing* or *equalising*

equation
mathematical statement that 2 expressions are equal

equip
to provide with what is necessary
equipped equipping

equipment
tools, etc., necessary for a task or activity

equity
fairness

a b c d e f g h i j k l m n o p q r s t u v w x y z

equivalent
equal in value or significance
equivalence

era
period in history

erase
to rub out
eraser erasing

erect
upright; to construct
erection erector

error
mistake or inaccuracy
err erring erroneous

erupt
(*of a volcano*) to shoot out lava, etc., suddenly; to break out fiercely
eruption

escape
to break free
escapee escaper escaping *escapism escapist*

especially
particularly

essay
written composition; (*formal*) to attempt
essays essayed essayist

essence
basic intrinsic nature

essential
necessary; basic
essentially

establish
to set up; to settle
establishes

establishment
setting up (of); institution or business; most important people in a country

estate
landed property

estimate
(to make an) approximate calculation
estimating estimation estimator

eternal
lasting for ever
eternally eternity

ethics
study of morality; moral principles
ethical ethically

ethnic
of people grouped according to common features
ethnically

evaluate
to determine the value, significance, etc., of
evaluating evaluation

even
flat; level; still

evening
time of day from late afternoon to nightfall

event
incident; happening; contest in a sports programme
eventful

eventual
happening in the course of time
eventuality eventualities eventually

ever
always; at any time

every
each one; all

everybody
all the people

everyday
common; ordinary

everyone
all the people

everything
all the things

everywhere
in all places

evidence
something that gives reasons for belief or disbelief; sign or indication

evident
obvious; clear
evidently

evil
(something) bad or wicked

evolution
process of gradual development
evolutionary evolve evolving

exact
correct; precise; to force people to give, esp. money
exaction exactitude exactly

exaggerate
to represent as greater, more important, more successful, etc., than is true
exaggerating exaggeration

exam
(informal) short for **examination**

examination
examining; test of a person's knowledge or skill

examine
to put questions to in order to test knowledge or skill; to look at closely
examinee examiner examining

example
something that is typical of its group or worthy of imitation
exemplary exemplify

exceed
to be greater than; to go beyond
exceedingly

excellent
extremely good
excellence

except
not including; apart from; to exclude
excepting

exception
something that is different from most others of its kind

exceptional
unusual; extremely good
exceptionally

excerpt
extract from a book, speech, etc.

excess
amount that is more than a certain, esp. normal or permitted, limit
excessive excessively

exchange
to give or transfer in return for something else
exchangeable exchanging

excite
to arouse the feelings of
excitable excited exciting

excitement
feeling of being lively and happy, esp. when waiting for something to happen

exclaim
to cry out suddenly and with strong feeling
exclamation exclamatory

exclude
to reject; to shut out from
excluding exclusion

exclusive
having the right to exclude; restricted; very fashionable; not including

excuse
to pardon; to free from blame; reason given for excusing a fault
excusable excusing

execute
to carry out fully; to put to death as a legal punishment
executing execution executioner

executive
part of government that administers a country's laws; person with managerial or administrative power

exercise
set of questions designed to develop a skill; activity for training the body or mind; to make use of; to train
exercising

exhaust
to tire out; to use up completely; waste gas or vapour ejected from an engine
exhaustible exhaustion

exhibit
to display to the public; item on display to the public
exhibition exhibitor

exhilarate
to make lively
exhilarating exhilaration

exile
long enforced absence from one's country, etc.; to banish in this way; exiled person
exilic exiling

exist
to be; to live
existence existent

exit
way out; (*Latin*) stage direction for actor to leave the stage

exorbitant
excessive

expand
to make or become larger
expansion expansive

expanse
wide area over which something is spread out

expect
to consider probable; to look forward to
expectancy expectant expectation

expend
to spend or use up
expendable expenditure

expense
spending of money; amount of money spent

expensive
costing or charging a lot of money

experience
awareness or knowledge of something; skills and abilities learned; to feel
experiencing

experiment
(to conduct an) investigation; to test a hypothesis; trial arrangement
experimental experimentation experimenter

expert
(someone) with great skill or knowledge
expertise

explain
to make plain or clear; to show the meaning of; to give reasons for
explanation explanatory explicable

explode
to burst noisily and with force
exploding

exploit
to take unfair advantage of
exploitation exploitative

explore
to travel through unfamiliar areas to make geographical discoveries; to investigate
exploration exploratory explorer exploring

explosion
act of bursting with a loud noise and great force
explosive

export
to send goods or services to a foreign country; something exported
exportation exporter

expose
to uncover or reveal
exposing exposure

express
to make known; to show; definitely stated; of or designed for quick travel or delivery
expressible expression expressive

extend
to reach; to stretch out
extended extension extensive

extent
range, area, or length

exterior
outer (surface or part)

external
of or for the outside; outward; of the foreign affairs of a country

extinct
no longer existing; (*of a volcano*) not likely to erupt
extinction

extra
additional

extraordinary
unusual; remarkable
extraordinarily extraordinariness

extreme
in a very high degree; point that is as far from another point or the centre as it is possible to be
extremely extremism extremist extremity extremities

extrovert
person whose attention is directed towards interests outside himself or herself
extroverted

exuberant
very lively
exuberance

eye
organ of sight; to watch closely
eyed eyeing or eying

eyebrow
curved line of hair above the eye

Ff

fabric
cloth, structure

face
front of head; to be looking in the direction of
facing

facility
ease; room or equipment for a particular purpose
facilities

fact
something known to have happened
factual factuality

factor
element or condition; agent; (maths) one of the numbers that when multiplied together make a product
factorial factorize or factorise

factory
place where goods are manufactured
factories

faculty
ability or power of the mind or body; university or college department
faculties

fade
to (cause to) lose colour, freshness, or clarity
fading

fail
to (declare to) be unsuccessful; to break down; to disappoint
failing

failure
lack of success; breakdown

faint
weak; to lose consciousness

fair[1]
light in colour; just; fine; beautiful

fair[2]
market; collection of entertainments; trade exhibition

fairly
in a fair way; quite

fairy
small imaginary being
fairies

faith
trust; belief

faithful
loyal; accurate
faithfully

fall
to drop down; act of dropping down; decrease; (US) autumn
fallen fell

false
incorrect; untrue
falsehood falsely falsity

fame
reputation; renown

familiar
well-known; acquainted (with)
familiarity familiarities familiarize or *familiarise*

family
parents and their children; group of similar or closely related things
families

famous
very well-known

fan[1]
(device) to create a current of air
fanned fanning

fan[2]
fanatical supporter

fancy
to imagine; to have a liking for; playful imagination; elaborate
fancies fancied fancier fanciest fanciful fancying

fantastic
great; strange
fantastically

fantasy
something imagined, esp. wild or extravagant
fantasies

far
distant; to a considerable extent

fare
money charged for a journey; food and drink; to get on
faring

farm
area of land for growing crops or raising animals
farmer

farther
at or to a greater distance; more
farthest

fascinate
to hold the interest of
fascinating fascination

fashion
style, esp. of clothes; way of doing something; to form

fashionable
stylish
fashionably

fast
quick; firmly fixed

fasten
to tie or attach

fat
soft greasy substance, esp. in animal bodies; overweight
fatted fatten fatter fattest fattier fattiest fatty

fatal
resulting in death
fatality fatalities

fate
power predetermining events; destiny
fateful

father
(to be a) male parent; priest or leader
fatherhood father-in-law fathers-in-law

fatigue
tiredness; weakness in metals; to make or become tired
fatiguing

fault
mistake; flaw; break in the earth's crust
faultier faultiest faultless faulty

favour (US **favor**)
to like or support; helpful act

favourable (US **favorable**)
advantageous; approving
favourably (US *favorably*)

favourite (US **favorite**)
preferred (thing or person)
favouritism (US *favoritism*)

fax
machine that sends and receives documents along a telephone line; document sent in this way; to send in this way
faxes

fear
feeling caused by danger, pain, or evil; to be afraid of
fearful fearless fearsome

feather
flat light structure on a bird's skin

feature
prominent part, esp. of the face; special article in a magazine, etc.; to play a part in; to give prominence to
featuring

February
2nd month of the year

federal
having power divided between central and regional government
federalism federalist federate federating federation

fee
payment

feed
to give food to
fed

feel
to examine by touch; to experience
felt

feeling
sense or sensation; emotion
feelingly

feet
pl. of foot

fell
past tense of fall

fellow
man or boy; boyfriend; person or comrade; member of a college or institution
fellowship

felt[1]
past tense and past participle of feel

felt[2]
fabric made from compressing wool, hair, etc.

female
(of the) sex that conceives and bears offspring

feminine
of women or qualities thought to be womanly
femininity feminism feminist

fence
(to surround with a) barrier; to fight with a sword or foil
fencing

ferry
(boat) to transport across a river or channel
ferries ferried ferrying

fertile
capable of producing offspring, crops, etc.; productive
fertility fertilize or *fertilise fertilizer* or *fertiliser*

festival
celebration; series of special events
festive festivity festivities

fetch
to go for and bring or take back; to bring in a price
fetches

fever
disease marked by high body temperature
feverish

few
not many

fiancé (fem. **fiancée**)
person one is engaged to be married to

fibre (US **fiber**)
fine thread; fabric made from such thread
fibrous

fiction
something invented; invented story
fictional fictionalize or *fictionalise fictitious*

field
open land; area; to stop and return a ball

fierce
violently cruel; intense

fifteen
number 15
fifteenth

fifty
number 50
fifties fiftieth fifty-fifty

fight
(to) struggle
fought

figure
symbol of a number; to reckon or consider
figuring

file
(to place in a) folder for holding papers; line of people; steel tool used for smoothing
filing

fill
to make or become full; all that is needed to fill

film
flexible material used in photography; (to make a) sequence of photographs; thin layer
filmic filmy

filter
(to purify with or use a) strainer

filthy
very dirty; obscene
filth filthier filthiest filthiness

final
coming last; conclusive
finalist finality finalize or *finalise finally*

finance
management of money; to provide money for
financier financing

financial
of or with regard to money
financially

find
to discover; to obtain; (law) to declare
found

fine[1]
of very good quality; clear; delicate
finer finery finest

fine[2]
(to punish by imposing a) financial penalty
fining

finger
one of the parts extending from the hand

finish
(to bring or come to an) end
finishes

fire
heat and light given off in burning; to shoot; (informal) to dismiss
fiery firing

fireplace
place where a fire burns to heat a room

firm
solid; steady; business company

first
(coming) at the beginning

fiscal
of government finance

fish
(to try to catch a) cold-blooded animal living in water
fish or *fishes*

fisherman
man who catches fish
fishermen

fist
hand with fingers tightly closed in pal

fit[1]
suitable; ready; healthy; to make suitable for
fitted fitter fittest fitting

fit[2]
sudden attack or convulsion
fitful

five
number 5
fifth fiver

fix
to make firm; to repair; to decide
fixable fixed fixes fixture

flag
banner with a special design

flame
bright tongue-shaped part of a fire; to burn with flames
flaming

flap
to move up and down or from side to side; material used to cover an opening
flapped flapping

flash
(to give out a) sudden short blaze of light
flashes

flat
level and smooth; (of a musical note) lower by a semitone; self-contained set of rooms on one floor
flatter flattest flattish

flavour (US **flavor**)
taste perceived in the mouth; (to add a) substance used to give a special taste

flee
to run away from
fled fleeing

fleet
group of warships under one command

flesh
soft substance of the body, esp. muscular parts
fleshy

flew
past tense of **fly**[1]

flexible
able to be bent easily without breaking
flexibility

flight
movement through the air; set of stairs; act of running away

float
to (cause to) rest on the surface of a liquid; something such as a cork that is designed to float; low flat lorry; sum of money

flock
group of animals or birds; to gather or move in a group or crowd

flood
overflowing of water; overwhelming quantity; to cover with a flood

floor
lower surface of a room; bottom of the sea; storey of a building

flour
powdered grain of wheat, etc., used in baking

flow
to move freely and smoothly; steady movement

flower
part of a plant that produces seeds; (to) blossom

flown
past participle of **fly**[1]

flu
virus disease marked by fever, aches, and pains, etc.

fluent
able to speak a particular foreign language easily
fluency

fluorescent
emitting light
fluoresce fluorescence

fly[1]
to move through the air, esp. by wings; flap over an opening
flies flew flier or *flyer flown flying*

fly[2]
2-winged insect
flies

focus
point of convergence of light rays; point at which an object is seen most clearly; to bring or come into focus
focuses or *foci focal focused* or *focussed focusing* or *focussing*

fog
(to cover with a) thick mist that is difficult to see through
fogged fogging foggier foggiest foggy

fold
to bend so that one part covers the other; folded part

folk
people; (informal) family

follow
to go or come after; to pursue; to understand

following
coming after or next; group of *followers*

fond
having a liking for; affectionate

food
substance taken into the body and used to provide energy

fool
person without good sense
foolish

foot
lowest part of leg; lowest part of something; unit of length, 12 inches; basic unit in poetry
feet footage

football
team game in which kicking the ball plays a major role

footstep
sound or mark made by foot when walking

for
used to show purpose or direction; intended to be given to; considering; because (of); on behalf of

forbid
to prohibit
forbade or *forbad forbidden forbidding*

force
strength, energy, or power; powerful thing, person, or group; to compel
forceful forcible forcing

forecast
to predict future events; prediction
forecast or *forecasted*

forehead
part of the face above the eyes

foreign
from another country, esp. not in or of one's own country
foreigner

forest
large wooded area with dense growth of trees
forestry

forever or **for ever**
for all time in the future; constantly

forfeit
to lose the right to something as a penalty; something lost or removed as a penalty
forfeiture

forge
workshop with an open furnace; to shape metal by heat; to counterfeit; to move ahead steadily
forger forgery forgeries forging

forget
to fail to remember; to disregard
forgetful forgettable forgetting forgot forgotten

forgive
to stop blaming; to pardon
forgave forgivable forgiven forgiveness forgiving

fork
pronged implement; place where road, etc., separates into 2 or more parts

form
shape or appearance; paper with spaces to be filled in; school class; to shape
formative

formal
polite; conventional
formality formalities formalize or *formalise formally*

format
size, shape, and appearance of a book, etc.; to give a particular format to
formatted formatting

formation
forming; arrangement in a special pattern

former
of an earlier or previous time; first of 2 mentioned
formerly

formula
scientific rule made up of symbols; fixed set of words; statement of principle
formulas or *formulae*

forth
onwards; out
forthcoming

fortnight
2 weeks
fortnightly

fortunate
lucky
fortunately

fortune
luck, esp. good luck; large sum of money

forty
number 40
forties fortieth

forward
ahead; for the future; to send on; eager; mainly attacking player in soccer, etc.
forwards

fought
past tense and past participle of **fight**

found[1]
past tense and past participle of **find**

found[2]
to establish; to base
founder

foundation
act of founding or establishing; strong bottom section on which something is built

fountain
spring of water; jet of water

four
number 4
fourth

fourteen
number 14
fourteenth

fox
wild flesh-eating animal; to perplex or puzzle
foxes foxy

fragment
broken-off part or piece; to break into fragments
fragmentary fragmentation

frame
structure that gives shape or strength; outer structure; to put a frame round
framing

framework
supporting structure; set of basic ideas, principles, rules, etc.

frank
direct and honest; to mark a letter to cancel a stamp or instead of a stamp
frankly

fraud
deliberate deception; person who deceives
fraudulence fraudulent

free
not under the control of another; costing or charging nothing
freely

freedom
state of being not under another's control; right to do something

freeze
to change from a liquid into a solid because of a fall in temperature
froze frozen

freight
transport of goods; goods transported

frequent
occurring or appearing often; to visit often
frequency frequencies frequently

fresh
new; original; most recent; not canned, frozen, or preserved; invigorating
freshen

Friday
6th day of the week

fridge
(informal) short for refrigerator

fried
past tense and past participle of **fry**

friend
person whom one knows and likes
friendship

a b c d e f g h i j k l m n o p q r s t u v w x y z

friendly
pleasant and helpful
friendlier friendliest friendliness

fright
sudden fear or shock
frightful

frighten
to make suddenly afraid
frightened frightening

from
used to show an original location; out of; because of

front
forward part; promenade by the seashore
frontage frontal

frontier
border between 2 countries

frost
weather when the temperature falls below freezing-point;
white deposit of ice particles
frostier frostiest frostily frosty

frown
to wrinkle the brows

froze
past tense of **freeze**

frozen
past participle of **freeze**

fruit
part of plant containing seed; product or result
fruiterer fruitier fruitiest fruition fruity

fruitful
productive

fry
to cook in hot fat
fried fries frying

fuel
(to provide with) material burnt to produce light, heat, or energy
fuelled (US *fueled*)
fuelling (US *fueling*)

fulfil (US **fulfill**)
to carry out; to achieve
fulfilled fulfilling fulfilment
(US *fulfillment*)

full
completely filled;
completely satisfied
fuller fullest fullness
or *fulness fully*

fun
amusement, entertainment, or sport

function
to operate; purpose for activity; ceremony
functional

fund
supply of money for a purpose; store or supply; to provide money for

fundamental
basic or primary
(fact or principle)
fundamentally

funeral
formal ceremony at which a dead person is buried or cremated
funereal

funny
amusing; peculiar
funnier funniest funnily funniness

fur
soft thick hair of many animals
furred furrier furring furry

furnish
to provide with furniture; to provide or equip
furnishes

furniture
movable articles such as chairs that equip a house

further
to a greater distance or degree; in addition; to promote
furtherance furthest

fuse
length of wire in an electric circuit; length of material for setting off an explosive charge; to unite (as if) by melting together
fusible fusing fusion

fuss
excessive or unnecessary excitement or agitation; display or great affection; to show excessive concern or worry for
fusses fussier fussiest fussily fussy

future
(of or in the) time to come
futuristic futurity futurology

a b c d e f g h i j k l m n o p q r s t u v w x y z

Gg

gadget
small mechanical device
gadgetry

gain
to acquire; to profit; (to) increase
gainful

gallery
covered passage; balcony; upper floor in a theatre, etc.; room or building for displaying works of art
galleries

gallon
unit of liquid measurement, 4 *quarts*

gallop
(of a horse) (to go at the) fastest speed
galloped galloping

gamble
to risk money on the outcome of an event; to play games for money
gambler gambling

game
form of amusement or sport; scheme; wild animals hunted for sport or food; to gamble; brave
gaming

gang
group of criminals; group of workers

gaol see **jail**

gap
break, opening, or interruption

garage
building for a motor vehicle; commercial establishment where cars are repaired or sold or where petrol, etc., is sold
garaging

garden
area of land where trees, flowers, vegetables, etc., are growing; to cultivate a garden
gardener

gas
airlike substance; to poison or affect with gas
gases gassed gassing gassy

gasp
to catch one's breath sharply; act of gasping

gate
movable barrier for closing an opening in a wall or fence

gather
to bring or come together

gauge
(device or instrument with which) to measure, test, or estimate
gaugeable gauging

gave
past tense of **give**

gay
(informal) homosexual; cheerful; bright
gaiety gaily gayer gayest gayness

gaze
to look at long and steadily
gazing

gear
toothed wheel in a mechanism; mechanism or equipment

geese
pl. of **goose**

gender
state of being male or female; grammatical category of nouns, esp. masculine, feminine, and neuter

gene
unit of heredity in a chromosome

general
of the whole; not limited; chief army officer
generality generalities *generalization* or *generalisation generalize* or *generalise generally*

generate
to produce or create
generating generator

generation
generating; group of people born at about the same time

generic
of a whole class or group
generically

generous
giving readily and liberally
generosity

genetics
study of heredity
genetic genetically geneticist

gentle
not severe; mild or kind
gently

gentleman
man
gentlemen gentlemanly

genuine
not artificial; sincere or real

geography
study of the natural features of the earth's surface
geographer geographic geographical geographically

geology
study of structure, composition, etc., of the earth
geological geologically geologist

geometry
branch of mathematics dealing with the measurements and properties of angles, lines, and surfaces
geometric geometrical geometrically

germ
micro-organism that can cause disease

gesture
(to make a) movement, esp. of the hands or arms, to express a feeling or for emphasis
gestured gesturing

get
to obtain or receive; to become; to move
getting got (US) *gotten*

ghost
disembodied spirit of a dead person
ghostliness ghostly

giant
very large (person or thing)

gift
something given; talent
gifted

giggle
to laugh foolishly; such a laugh
giggling

giraffe
long-necked African animal

girl
young unmarried human female
girlfriend girlhood girlish

give
to hand over; to make a present of; to yield under pressure
gave given giver giving

glad
pleased; happy
gladden gladder gladdest gladly gladness

glance
to look at quickly; to strike lightly and obliquely; quick look
glancing

glass
hard brittle transparent substance; something made of this such as a drinking container
glasses glassy

glide
to move along smoothly
glider gliding

glimpse
to see briefly; brief look
glimpsing

global
concerning the whole world
globe

gloom
darkness; sadness
gloomier gloomiest gloomily gloominess gloomy

glory
praise or honour
glories glorify glorious

glove
hand covering with parts for each finger

glow
(to shine with a) bright steady light

glue
(to join with a) strong adhesive
glued gluey gluing

go
to move or travel; to operate; to become
goes going gone went

goal
aim; structure into which players put the ball, etc., to score

goat
kind of horned ruminant mammal

god (fem. **goddess**) (**God**)
supreme being; image or idol that is worshipped
godly

gold
valuable yellow metal
golden of gold; favourable

golf
game played with a ball and clubs on a large open course

gone
past participle of **go**

good
of a high standard; favourable; pleasing; well-behaved; virtuous; benefit
best better

goodbye (US **goodby**)
farewell

goods
movable or manufactured items

goodwill
kindly feeling; favour that a business has gained

goose
kind of large long-necked, web-footed bird
geese

gorgeous
magnificent and beautiful

gorilla
largest manlike ape

gossip
(to engage in) idle or malicious talk about other people; person who does this
gossiped gossiping

got
past tense and past participle of **get**

govern
to direct and control
governable governance governess governor

government
executive policy-making body of a country
governmental

grab
to grasp hastily or roughly
grabbed grabbing

grace
elegance or beauty in movement or expression; kindness or favour; to add elegance or beauty to
graceful gracing gracious

grade
level in a scale of qualities, value, or ranks; to arrange in a scale; (to give a) mark to students' work
gradation grading

gradual
proceeding by steps; not abrupt
gradually

graduate
to receive an academic degree; someone who has graduated; to mark with units of measurement
graduating graduation

grain
(small seed or fruit of a) cereal grass; general pattern or texture in wood, etc.
grainy

gram or **gramme**
metric unit of weight

grammar
study of the structure of sentences, esp. regarding conformity to stated rules
grammatical grammatically

grand
large and important; impressive; very good
grandeur

grandchild
child of one's son or daughter

granddaughter
daughter of one's son or daughter

grandfather
father of one's mother or father

grandmother
mother of one's mother or father

grandparent
parent of one's mother or father

grandson
son of one's son or daughter

grant
to allow or give; something given

grape
juicy berry of the vine

grasp
(to) grip; to understand; understanding

grass
spreading plant with long narrow green leaves
grasses grassy

grateful
feeling or showing thanks
gratefully gratitude

grave[1]
place for burying a corpse

grave[2]
serious, earnest
gravely gravity

grease
(to apply an) oily substance
greasy

great
relatively large; eminent
greatly greatness

greedy
having a great desire, esp. for food
greed greedier greediest greedily greediness

green
colour between blue and yellow; immature and inexperienced; protecting the environment

greet
to address with words of welcome
greeting

grew
past tense of grow

grey (US **gray**)
colour between white and black

grief
deep sorrow
grievance grieve grieving grievous

grill
to cook under or over direct heat; framework for cooking on; to question intensely

grim
stern; harsh
grimmer grimmest

grind
to crush into fine particles
grinder ground

grip
to hold firmly
gripped gripping

groan
(to utter a) deep sound of pain, disapproval, etc.

gross
outrageous; bulky; whole amount, not net; coarse; 144
grossly

ground[1]
surface of the earth; area; soil; reason

ground[2]
past tense and past participle of **grind**

group
number of people or things together or having a common feature

grow
to increase in size, etc.; to become mature; to become; to raise
grew grown growth

growl
(to make a) low rumbling threatening sound

grown
past participle of grow

grown-up
adult

growth
growing; increase; something that has grown, esp. on something else

guarantee
(to give a) formal promise or undertaking
guaranteed guaranteeing guarantor

guard
to watch over and protect or look after; person that guards

guardian
person legally entrusted with the care of another

guerrilla or guerilla
member of a small independent armed force

guess
(to form or express an) opinion or estimate without full knowledge or calculation
guesses

guest
visitor

guide
person who leads the way; to lead; member of girls' movement
guidance guiding

guilt
feeling that one is to blame; fact of having done wrong

guilty
having done wrong
guiltier guiltiest guiltily guiltiness

guitar
kind of plucked stringed instrument
guitarist

gum
sticky substance exuded by certain plants; fleshy tissue covering the base of the teeth; to stick
gummed gumming gummy

gun
kind of firearm
gunner gunning

a b c d e f g h i j k l m n o p q r s t u v w x y z

gut
(lower part of the) alimentary canal; to remove the entrails from; to destroy the inside of a building
gutted gutting

guy
(informal) man; effigy of Guy Fawkes

gym
gymnasium; gymnastics

Hh

habit
usual manner or behaviour; costume of a monk or nun
habitual habitually habituate

habitat
natural environment of an animal or plant

had
past tense and past participle of **have**
hadn't

haddock
kind of sea-fish, smaller than cod

hail[1]
small pellets of ice

hail[2]
to greet enthusiastically; to have come (from)

hair
thread-like structure growing from the skin
hairy

haircut
act of cutting someone's hair; style in which one's hair is cut

hairdresser
person who cuts and styles hair

half
either of two equal parts
halves halfway

hall
passage at the entrance of a house or building; large room for public meetings; mansion

hallo see **hello**

halt
(to bring or come to a) stop

halve
to divide into two equal parts
halving

ham
(meat from the) hind leg of a pig; (informal) amateur radio operator; (informal) to overact
hammed hamming

hammer
tool with a heavy head for driving in nails, etc.

hamper[1]
to hinder the progress or movement of

hamper[2]
large covered basket and the food inside it

hand
part of the arm at the end of the wrist; pointer on a clock; manual worker; cards dealt to a player; to give with the hand

handbag
woman's small bag for carrying personal items

handful
amount that can be held in one hand; small number

handicap
disability; to put at a disadvantage
handicapped handicapping

handkerchief
small piece of cloth for wiping the nose
handkerchiefs or *handkerchieves*

handle
part of an object designed to be held in order to move, lift, etc., the object; to touch with the hands; to deal with
handler handling

handsome
good-looking; generous

handy
convenient; skilful with the hands
handier handiest handily handiness

hang
to fix to a point so that the lower part is free (past tense and past participle **hung**); to put to death by suspending from a rope (past tense and past participle **hanged**)

happen
to occur
happening

happy
glad or pleased; fortunate
happier happiest happily happiness

harass
to trouble by persistent attacks
harasses harassment

harbour (US **harbor**)
port for ships; to keep in the mind

hard
firm or tough; difficult; requiring great energy; harsh; with considerable force

hardly
scarcely

hardware
tools and implements for use in the home; the mechanical and electronic parts of a computer

harm
to damage or injure; damage or injury
harmful harmless

harmony
agreement; pleasing combination of sounds
harmonies harmonic harmonious harmonize or *harmonise*

harsh
rough, severe, or cruel

harvest
(to gather in) ripened crops; season when this is done; result of effort

has
3rd person sing. of present tense of **have**
hasn't

haste
speed; hurry
hasten hastily hastiness hasty

hat
head covering, esp. with brim and crown

hate
(to feel an) intense dislike
hateful hating hatred

haul
to pull with effort; to transport; amount obtained
haulage haulier

haunt
(of ghosts) to frequent

have
to possess or obtain; to hold
had has haven't

hay
cut and dried grass or clover used to feed animals

hazard
(source of) risk or danger; to risk
hazardous

he
subject pronoun referring to a male person or animal

head
part of the body containing the eyes, ears, brain, etc.; upper or front part; leader or director; to move towards

headache
pain in the head

heading
title

headline
heading, esp. of a newspaper story

headmaster
(fem. headmistress)
most senior teacher in charge of a school

headquarters
place from which an organization is controlled

heal
to make or become healthy
healer

health
condition of body or mind; being well

healthy
in good, esp. physical condition
healthier healthiest healthiness

heap
(to put in a) pile of things lying one on top of the other

hear
to perceive sound with the ear; to pay attention to
heard hearer hearing

heart
organ that pumps blood round the body; love; central part of something
hearty

heat
being hot; to make or become hot; preliminary stage in a competition
heated heater heating

heaven
dwelling-place of God; place of greatest happiness; sky
heavenly

heavy
weighty; difficult; hard
heavier heaviest heavily heaviness

he'd
(informal) he would; he had

hedge
row of densely growing bushes; to avoid giving a straight answer

heel
back part of the foot below the ankle

height
distance measured from the bottom to the top of something; high area
heighten

heir (fem. **heiress**)
person who inherits or is entitled to inherit

held
past tense and past participle of **hold**

helicopter
aircraft with horizontally rotating blades

hell
dwelling-place of the Devil; place of punishment or extreme misery; (informal) exclamation of anger, etc.
hellish

he'll
(informal) he will

hello, hallo, or **hullo** exclamation used in greeting, attracting attention, etc.

helmet
defensive or protective head-covering
helmeted

help
(to) aid or support
help helper helpful helpless

hen
female bird; chicken

her
object or possessive form of she

herb
plant used in cooking and medicine
herbal

here
in or to this place; at or to this point

heredity
transmission of genetic factors from one generation to the next
hereditary

hero (fem. **heroine**)
very courageous person; main person in a play, etc.
heroes heroic heroically *heroism*

hers
(the one or ones) belonging to *her*

herself
reflexive form of **she**

he's
(informal) he is; he has

hesitate
to be slow or reluctant in speech or action
hesitancy hesitant hesitating hesitation

heterosexual
sexually attracted to people of the opposite sex

hey
exclamation used to show discovery, surprise, etc.

hi
(informal) hello

hide[1]
to put or keep out of sight; place for observing animals and birds
hid hidden hiding

hide[2]
animal's skin

hideous
very ugly

hierarchy
system arranged in ranks
hierarchies hierarchical

high
reaching far from bottom to top; far above the ground; above normal; raised in pitch
higher highest highly

highlight
to emphasize

highway
main road

hill
natural rise in ground
hillier hilliest hilly

him
object form of **he**

himself
reflexive form of **he**

hinder
to get in the way of
hindrance

hint
(to give a) brief suggestion

hip
side of the body where the legs join the trunk

hire
to pay for the temporary use of; to employ; payment for temporary use
hiring

his
possessive form of **he**; (the one or ones) belonging to him

hiss
(to make an) *s*-sound, expressing disapproval
hisses hissing

history
(study of) past events
histories historian historic *historical historically*

hit
(to deal a) blow; successful record, etc.
hitter hitting

hitch
to fasten with a hook, etc.; slight difficulty; to hitchhike
hitches

hoarse
harsh-sounding

hoax
to deceive as a trick or joke; such a deception
hoaxes

hobby
activity pursued in spare time
hobbies

hold
to keep in the hands or arms; to contain; space for cargo in a ship or aircraft
held

hole
(to make a) hollow space or opening in something
holey holing

holiday
period of rest from work

hollow
having empty space inside; sunken

holy
sacred; godly
holier holiest holiness

home
place where one lives

homeless
having no home

homework
work to be done at home by schoolchildren; preparation

homosexual
sexually attracted to people of one's own sex

honest
truthful or trustworthy; fair
honestly honesty

honey
syrup made by bees from nectar

honorary
conferred as an honour

honour (US **honor**)
(to) respect; reputation; privilege

honourable (US **honorable**)
moral and just; that can be admired
honourably (US *honorably*)

hook
(to fasten with a) curved piece of metal, etc., used to hang, catch, or pull something

hop
(to) jump, esp. on one foot
hopped hopping

hope
(to feel) expectant desire for something
hopeful hopefully hopeless hoping

horizon
line at which earth and sky appear to meet

horizontal
parallel to the horizon
horizontally

horn
pointed bony growth on the head of some animals; musical instrument; warning device on a vehicle, etc.

horrible
very unpleasant
horribly

horror
feeling of terror
horrid horrific horrify

horse
4-footed animal with mane and tail, used for riding, etc.; to play (around)
horsing horsy

hospital
place where the sick and injured are treated
hospitalize or *hospitalise*

host (fem. **hostess**)
person who welcomes guests into his or her home

hostage
person held as a security that certain terms will be met

hostile
opposed; unfriendly; antagonistic
hostility hostilities

hot
having a high temperature
hotter hottest

hotel
commercial establishment providing food and rooms for travellers
hotelier

hour
24th part of a day
hourly

house
building for people to live in; to provide accommodation for
housing

household
people who live together in one dwelling

housewife
woman whose main work is to look after a house and family
housewives

housework
work of keeping a house clean

how
in what way; to what extent

however
to whatever extent; nevertheless

huge
very large

hullo see **hello**

hum
(to make a) low continuous vibrating sound
hummed humming

human
person; of people
humanity humanities

humane
kind; sympathetic

humble
not proud; submissive; to cause to feel humble
humbler humblest humbling humbly humility

humid
moist
humidifier humidify humidity

humiliate
to hurt someone's pride
humiliating humiliation

humour (US **humor**)
funniness; temper; to indulge
humorist humorous

hump
round projection

hundred
number 100
hundredth

a b c d e f g h i j k l m n o p q r s t u v w x y z

hung
past tense and past participle of
hang

hungry
feeling a lack of food; eager
hunger hungrier hungriest hungrily

hunt
to search for; to pursue and kill
hunter hunting

hurry
to (cause to) go faster than usual
hurried hurries hurrying

hurt
to injure; to feel pain; (to) harm
hurtful

husband
man a woman is married to;
to use economically

hut
small rough house or shelter

hydrogen
gas that is the simplest, lightest, and most abundant element in the universe
hydrogenous

hygiene
maintenance of health; cleanliness
hygienic hygienically

hymn
song of praise, esp. to God

hyphen
punctuation mark - used to join words
hyphenate

hypocrisy
pretence of good standards or beliefs
hypocrite hypocritical hypocritically

hypothesis
provisional suggested explanation
hypotheses hypothetical hypothetically

hysteria
intense uncontrollable emotion or excitement
hysterical hysterically hysterics

Ii

I
subject pronoun referring to the person who is speaking or writing

ice
frozen water; to form ice
icier iciest icing icy

ice cream
frozen sweet creamy food

I'd
(informal) I had; I would; I should

idea
conception or notion

ideal
(something considered) perfect; existing only in the mind
idealism idealist idealistic idealistically

identical
being the same; exactly alike

identify
to determine or show the identity of; to associate oneself (with)
identification identified identifies identifying

identity
being identical; features of someone's personality, etc.
identities

idiom
expression that cannot be fully understood from the meaning of the words it contains
idiomatic idiomatically

idiot
stupid person
idiocy idiotic idiotically

idle
lazy; not used
idler idlest idling idly

idol
object of worship
idolater idolatry idolize or *idolise idolization* or *idolisation*

if
in the event that; whether
iffier iffiest iffy

ignorance
lack of knowledge
ignoramus ignoramuses ignorant

ignore
to refuse to notice; to fail to notice
ignoring

I'll
(informal) I will; I shall

ill
unwell; bad

illegal
forbidden by law
illegality illegalities illegally

illegible
unable to be read
illegibility illegibly

illness
disease or sickness; bad health

illusion
misleading impression
illusionist illusive illusory

illustrate
to provide with pictures or drawings; to explain by examples
illustrating illustration illustrator

I'm
(informal) I am

image
representation; optical appearance; mental picture
imagery

imaginary
not real; existing in the *imagination*

imagination
part of the mind that forms mental pictures and creates new ideas

imaginative
showing creative mental powers

imagine
to form a picture in the mind
imaginable imagining

imitate
to copy or mimic
imitating imitation imitative imitator

immediate
without delay; direct
immediacy immediately

immense
extremely large
immensity

immigrant
person who comes into and settles in a country
immigrate immigrating immigration

immobile
unable to move; motionless
immobility immobilize or *immobilise*

immoral
contrary to accepted morals
immorality

immune
not susceptible to something such as infection
immunity immunize or *immunise*

impact
(force of) collision of 2 things; impression; to fix firmly; to have an effect (on)

impair
to weaken or damage
impairment

impartial
fair; not biased
impartiality

impatient
not patient or tolerant
impatience

impeccable
flawless
impeccably

imperial
of an empire, emperor, or empress; sovereign; of British non-metric weights and measures
imperialism imperialist

impersonal
objective; not showing feelings

impersonate
to pretend to be another person
impersonating impersonation impersonator

implement
tool; to carry out; to put into action
implementation

implication
indirect suggestion; possible result

implicit
not expressed plainly; complete and unquestioning
implicitly

imply
to hint at indirectly
implied implies implying

impolite
not polite

import
to bring in goods or services from a foreign country; something imported; significance
importation importer

important
significant; authoritative
importance importantly

impose
to apply or enforce
imposing imposition

impossible
not possible
impossibility impossibilities *impossibly*

impress
to produce a deep effect on; to produce an imprint

impression
quickly formed or vague opinion; imprint
impressionable impressionism impressionist

impressive
striking; making a strong *impression*

imprint
(to) mark or print

imprison
to confine in prison
imprisonment

improve
to make or become better
improvement improving

impulse
sudden urgent drive or desire
impulsion impulsive

in
used to show a position in space; inside; (informal) fashionable

inability
lack of ability

inadequate
not adequate; unable to cope
inadequacy

inappropriate
not suitable

inaugurate
to begin or open formally
inaugurating inauguration

incentive
motivating influence; stimulus

inch
unit of length; one-twelfth of a foot
inches

incident
occurrence or event

incidental
happening as a result of something more important
incidentally

incline
(to cause) to lean or slope; slope; to tend
inclination inclining

include
to put as part of a larger group; to contain
including inclusion inclusive

income
amount of money gained, esp. from work

inconceivable
incapable of being conceived or imagined
inconceivability inconceivably

inconvenience
something that causes slight discomfort, etc.; to cause inconvenience to
inconveniencing inconvenient inconveniently

incorporate
to include as a part of a whole; to form a legal corporation
incorporating incorporation

incorrect
not correct

increase
to make or become greater
increasing increasingly

incredible
unbelievable; (informal) amazing
incredibility incredibly

incur
to bring upon oneself
incurred incurring

indeed
really; in fact

indefinite
not defined exactly
indefinitely

indelible
incapable of being erased
indelibly

independent
self-governing; objective; not dependent on others
independence independently

index
alphabetical list at the back of a book; pointer; number indicating changes in value
indexes or *indices*

indicate
to point or show
indicating indication indicator

indigo
deep-blue colour or dye

indirect
not direct

indispensable
essential

individual
one person or thing; separate
individualism individualist individuality individually

indoor
(taking place) inside a building
indoors

induce
to cause, persuade, or influence; to cause labour to begin; to draw a conclusion
inducement inducing induction inductive

indulge
to yield to the wishes of
indulgence indulgent indulging

industry
production of esp. manufactured goods; producers of a particular type of goods; hard work
industries industrial industrialist industrialize or *industrialise industrious*

inequality
lack of equality
inequalities

inevitable
that cannot be avoided
inevitability inevitably

infant
child in the earliest stage of its life
infancy infantile

infect
to affect with a disease
infection infectious

infer
to conclude by reasoning from facts
inference inferred inferring

inferior
(person who is) lower in rank or worth
inferiority

infinite
endless; immeasurable
infinitely infinity

inflate
to fill with gas or air
inflatable inflating

inflation
general rise in prices
inflationary

influence
(ability or power to produce an) effect; to affect
influencing influential

inform
to tell or communicate
informant informative informer

informal
not formal
informality informally

information
knowledge or facts about something

ingenious
clever or skilful
ingenuity

ingredient
one of the parts of a mixture, esp. in cooking

inhabit
to live in; to occupy
inhabitable inhabitant

inherit
to receive by legal right after someone's death; to receive by heredity
inheritance inheritor

inhibit
to restrain; to forbid or prevent
inhibition

initial
of the beginning; (to write the) first letter of a name or word
initialled (US *initialed*) *initialling* (US *initialing*) *initially*

initiate
to begin; to accept into a society with special ceremonies
initiating initiation initiator

initiative
first action; resourceful enterprise

inject
to introduce liquid into the body using a syringe; to introduce
injection

injure
to hurt, damage, or offend
injuring injurious

injury
physical damage or hurt
injuries

ink
coloured liquid for writing

inner
situated inside
innermost

innocent
not guilty; simple or naïve
innocence

innocuous
harmless

innovate
to introduce something new
innovating innovation innovator

inoculate
to introduce a micro-organism into; to vaccinate
inoculating inoculation

input
something put in, esp. supplied to a computer; to put in
inputting

inquiry
investigation
inquiries inquire inquiring

insect
small invertebrate animal with 6 legs and 2 pairs of wings

insecure
not confident
insecurity

inseparable
always together
inseparably

insert
to put in; something inserted
insertion

inside
(in or to the) inner part of something

insight
ability to perceive deeply

insist
to demand strongly
insistence insistent insistently

inspect
to examine very carefully, esp. for official purposes
inspection inspector

inspire
to act as a creative stimulus to
inspiration inspirational inspiring

install or **instal**
to place in position and make ready for use
installation installed installing

instalment
(US **installment**) part of a repayment; part of a series

instance
case or example

instant
moment; immediate; of the present month
instantly

instead
as an alternative or substitute

instil (US **instill**)
to introduce gradually
instilled instilling

instinct
inborn capacity or power
instinctive

institute
to establish or organize; organization for a particular purpose
instituting institution institutional

instruct
to teach, direct, or order
instruction instructive instructor

instrument
implement or tool; device that produces musical sounds

instrumental
of musical instruments; serving as a means for doing something
instrumentalist

insult
to speak to rudely and offensively; insulting utterance or action
insultingly

insurance
guarantee against risk, loss, etc.

insure
to take out insurance against; (US) to ensure
insured insurer insuring

intact
undamaged; complete

intake
taking in; people, things, etc., taken in

integral
essential to the whole

integrate
to form into a whole; to end esp. racial segregation
integrating integration

integrity
honesty; soundness

intellectual
relating to a person's capacity for serious thought; thinking person
intellect intellectualize or *intelletualise*

intelligence
mental ability; information about an enemy

intelligent
clever

intend
to propose; to design
intended

intense
extreme; deep
intensify intensity

intensive
marked by intensity; concentrated; thorough

intention
purpose or aim
intentional intentionally

interact
to act on each other
interaction interactive

intercede
to plead on behalf of another
interceding intercession intercessor

intercept
to stop, seize, or interrupt on the way
interception interceptor

interest
(to arouse a) sense of curiosity or concern; charge for borrowed money
interested interesting interestingly

interfere
to meddle or obstruct
interference interfering

interior
inner (surface or part); inland region

intermediate
between 2 points

internal
of or for the inside; inner; of the domestic affairs of a country

international
of 2 or more nations

Internet
worldwide network of computer links

interpret
to explain the meaning of
interpretation interpreter interpretive

interrogate
to ask questions intensely
interrogating interrogation interrogator

interrupt
to break in on; to break the flow of
interruption

interval
time or space between 2 events, etc.; (music) difference in pitch between 2 notes

intervene
to be or come between; to enter in order to stop a disagreement
intervening intervention

interview
formal discussion to assess an applicant for a job; questioning of a person for newspaper, television, etc.; to conduct an interview with
interviewee interviewer

into
to the inside of; to a different state, etc.

intrigue
to fascinate; to arouse the curiosity of; (to) plot
intrigued intriguer intriguing

introduce
to bring into use; to make (oneself or another person) known by name
introducing introduction introductory

introvert
person whose attention is concentrated on himself or herself
introverted

intrude
to force oneself on to or into without invitation
intruder intruding intrusion intrusive

invade
to enter a country, etc., by military force
invader invading invasion invasive

invalid[1]
sick or disabled person

invalid[2]
not valid
invalidate invalidity

invent
to create or originate; to produce
inventor invention inventive

invest
to commit money to a business expecting profit; to clothe or adorn (in robes of office, etc.)
investiture investment investor

investigate
to examine closely
investigating investigation investigative investigator

invisible
unable to be seen
invisibility

invite
to ask politely to come; to request
invitation inviting

involve
to include or entail; to associate; to make complicated
involved involvement involving

iron
metallic element that can be magnetized; (metal implement) to smooth or press clothes

irony
using words to express the opposite of the literal meaning
ironies ironic ironical ironically

irregular
not regular
irregularity

irrelevant
not relevant
irrelevance

irritate
to annoy; to make inflamed
irritable irritably irritating irritation

is
3rd person singular of present tense of be
isn't

island
land surrounded by water
islander

isolate
to place alone
isolating isolation

issue
flowing or sending out; edition of a magazine; offspring; topic; to bring or come out
issued issuing

it
subject or object pronoun referring to a thing or animal

item
single unit

itinerary
planned route for a journey
itineraries

it'll
(informal) it will

its
of it
itself

it's
(informal) it is; it has

I've
(informal) I have

ivy
kind of evergreen climbing plant
ivies

Jj

jack
device for raising heavy objects; playing-card, ranking just below a queen; electrical plug-in device; to raise with a jack

jacket
short outer garment

jail or **gaol**
(to send to) prison

jam[1]
preserve containing sweetened thickened fruit

jam[2]
(to) squeeze; to crowd; blockage
jammed jamming

January
1st month of the year

jar[1]
wide-mouthed cylindrical glass or earthenware container

jar[2]
(to make a) harsh discordant sound
jarred jarring

jaw
bony part holding the teeth

jazz
kind of music with syncopated rhythm; to make more lively

jealous
showing resentful suspicion of a rival; watchful and protecting
jealousy jealousies

jeans
close-fitting casual trousers

jelly
soft firm sweet made from gelatine; to make into or cover with a jelly
jellies jellied

jeopardize or **jeopardise**
to endanger
jeopardizing or *jeopardising jeopardy*

jersey
knitted garment for the upper part of the body
jerseys

jet
stream of liquid, gas, etc., forced through a narrow opening; aircraft powered by a jet engine; to rush out in a jet; to travel by jet
jetted jetting

jewel
precious stone
jewelled (US *jeweled*) *jeweller* (US *jeweler*) *jewellery* (chiefly US *jewelry*)

job
occupation, work, or task; to do occasional pieces of work
jobbed jobbing

jockey
rider in horse-races; to manoeuvre deviously
jockeys jockeyed jockeying

jog
to nudge slightly; to run slowly and steadily
jogged jogger jogging

join
to bring or come together; to become a member of
joiner joinery

joint
shared; place where two things join; large piece of cut meat

joke
funny anecdote; ridiculous circumstance
joking

jolly
(to make) merry or cheerful; (informal) very
jollied jollier jollies jolliest jollity jollying

journal
periodical or magazine; diary; record of book-keeping transactions

journalism
profession of reporting stories for the news media
journalist journalistic

journey
(to make a) trip
journeys journeyed journeying

joy
deep happiness
joyful joyless joyous

judge
public official with authority to decide legal cases; to hear and decide a legal case; to examine critically
judging

judgement or **judgment**
decision made by a judge; opinion reached by careful thought; ability to decide wisely
judgemental or *judgmental*

judicial
of justice or law-courts
judicially

judicious
having wise judgement

jug
container for pouring liquids; to stew hare, etc., in an earthenware container
jugged jugging

juice
natural liquid of a fruit, etc.
juicier juiciest juiciness juicy

July
7th month of the year

jumble
(to mix in a) confused disorder
jumbling

jump
to leap or spring clear of the ground; space or obstacle to be *jumped*

jumper
knitted garment for the upper part of the body

June
6th month of the year

jungle
tropical forest with a dense mass of vegetation

junior
(person) younger or lower in rank

junk
discarded articles; rubbish; (informal) to throw away

jury
people chosen to decide whether the accused is guilty or not

juries
just fair; deserved; righteous; only; not long since

justice
being just; administration of the law; title of a judge

justify
to prove or show to be right or just
justifiable justification justified justifies justifying

Kk

kangaroo
large Australian leaping marsupial

keen
eager; astute
keenly keenness

keep
to retain possession of; to remain; to look after; fort or castle
keeper kept

kennel
shelter for a dog; to keep in a kennel
kennelled (US *kenneled*) *kennelling* (US *kenneling*)

kerb (US **curb**)
stone, etc., edging of pavement

kettle
container for boiling water

key
shaped implement used to turn a lock or wind a mechanism; part pressed by finger on a piano, typewriter, etc.; system of related musical notes; most important

keyboard
set of keys on a piano, typewriter, or computer

kick
to hit or propel with the foot; act of kicking

kid[1]
young of a goat, etc.; leather from goatskin; young person
kiddie or *kiddy*

kid[2]
to tease; to deceive
kidded kidder kidding

kidnap
to seize and hold someone, esp. for ransom
kidnapped (US *kidnaped*) *kidnapper* (US *kidnaper*) *kidnapping* (US *kidnaping*)

kill
to cause the death of; to put an end to
killer killing

kilo
short for kilogram
kilos

kilogram or **kilogramme**
basic metric unit of mass; 1000 grams

kilometre (US **kilometer**)
1000 metres

kind[1]
friendly; helpful; generous
kindly
kindness kindnesses

kind[2]
group with common characteristics; type or sort

king
male sovereign ruler
kingly kingship

kingdom
territory ruled by a king or queen

kiss
(to) touch with the lips
kisses kissing

kit
(to provide with a) set of equipment, parts, or clothes
kitted kitting

kitchen
room where food is cooked

kite
light covered frame flown in the wind; bird of the hawk family

kitten
young cat

knee
joint between the thigh and lower leg

kneel
to rest or fall on the knees
kneeler kneeled or *knelt*

knew
past tense of know

knickers
woman's or girl's underpants

knife
cutting implement consisting of a sharp blade with handle
knives

knight
man with the title 'Sir'; chesspiece
knighthood

knit
to loop yarn or thread using long needles; to join closely
knitted knitting

knob
rounded handle

knock
(to hit with a) sharp blow; (to) rap

knot
fastening made by tying a piece of rope in a particular way; to tie or fasten in a knot; protuberance on a tree; speed of 1 nautical mile an hour
knotted knotting knotty

know
to be aware of; to understand or recognize
knew knowing known

knowledge
information known
knowledgeable knowledgeably

koala
Australian tree-dwelling marsupial

L

label
piece of material attached to an object to give information about it; to attach a label to
labelled (US *labeled*) *labelling* (US *labeling*)

laboratory
place where experiments are carried out
laboratories

laborious
marked by or needing great effort

labour (US **labor**)
work or exertion; process of childbirth; to work; workers
laboured (US *labored*) *labourer* (US *laborer*) *labouring* (US *laboring*)

lace
silk, linen, etc., fabric woven in a decorative open design; cord or string used to fasten a garment or shoe; to fasten with a lace; to add spirits to
lacing lacy

lack
insufficiency or shortage; to be short of

lad
boy

ladder
framework of 2 sidepieces joined by rungs used for climbing up and down; (to develop a) line of undone stitches

ladle
long-handled spoon with a deep bowl for serving liquids; to serve with a ladle
ladling

lady
woman; refined woman or woman of high social class; titled woman

ladies
lady-in-waiting ladies-in-waiting
ladylike ladyship

laid
past tense and past participle of **lay**[1]

lain
past participle of **lie**[2]

lake
large inland body of water

lamb
(meat of) young sheep

lamp
device that produces light

land
solid part of earth's surface; to come on to the shore or down from the air; country

landing
coming to land; floor area at the top of a flight of stairs

landlady
woman who lets property to tenants
landladies

landlord
man who lets property to tenants

landscape
(picture of an) area of scenery; to improve the natural features of a garden, etc.
landscaping

lane
narrow road or way

language
speech of a particular people; human speech

lap[1]
upper surface of the thighs of a seated person

lap[2]
one circuit of a racecourse; stage; to fold or wrap over
lapped lapping

lap[3]
to take in liquid with the tongue, as a cat does
lapped lapping

large
relatively great in size, area, scope, etc.
larger largest largish

largely
for the most part

laser
device generating a beam of high-intensity light

lass
girl or young woman
lasses

last[1]
coming at the end, after all others; most recent

last[2]
to continue for a period of time
lasting

late
coming after the expected or normal time; far on in the day or night; recently deceased
later latest

lately
recently

latter
second of 2 mentioned; nearer to the end

laugh
(to make the) sound expressing amusement
laughable laughter

launch
to move a vessel into the water; to propel with force; to cause to begin; act of launching; large motor boat
launches

laundry
place where clothes are washed and ironed; clothes that need to be washed
laundries launder launderette

lavatory
toilet
lavatories

law
authoritative rule of behaviour; legal profession
lawful lawless

a b c d e f g h i j k l m n o p q r s t u v w x y z

lawyer
person whose profession is to give advice on the law and represent people in legal cases

lay[1]
to put in a horizontal position; to produce eggs
laid laying

lay[2]
of people who are not clergy or not experts
layman laywoman

lay[3]
past tense of **lie**[2]

layer
thickness or covering; to arrange in layers
layered

layout
arrangement of something

lazy
not wanting to work
lazier laziest lazily laziness

lead[1]
to guide; to be in charge of; to be ahead in a contest
led

lead[2]
soft heavy metal; graphite in pencil
leaden

leader
person who guides or goes in front; person in charge
leadership

leading
first; principal

leaf
outgrowth from a plant stem; sheet of paper
leaves

leaflet
folded printed pamphlet giving information; to distribute leaflets in an area
leafleted leafleting

league
association or union; to form a league
leagued leaguing

leak
(hole or crack for a liquid) to escape or enter
leakage leaky

lean[1]
to (cause to) rest against a support
leaned or *leant leaning*

lean[2]
not fat; meagre
leanness

leap
(to) jump
leaped or *leapt leaping*

learn
to gain knowledge of or a skill in learned or learnt learner

learned
having a great knowledge
learning

lease
contract for the use of something, esp. property, for rent; to allow to use on payment of rent
leasing lessee lessor

least
smallest or slightest

leave[1]
to go away from; to cause to remain; to bequeath
leaving left

leave[2]
permission to do something; permission to be absent

lecture
(to give a) formal talk for instruction
lecturer lecturing

led
past tense and past participle of **lead**[1]

left[1]
past tense and past participle of **leave**[1]
left-overs

left[2]
opposite of right; having radical or socialist political views
leftist leftwards

leg
lower limb of animal on which it moves; stage in a journey or competition
legged

legacy
gift of money or property by will
legacies

legal
of the law; allowed by law
legality legalize or legalise legally

legend
old traditional story; inscription or title; explanation
legendary

legislate
to make laws
legislating legislation legislative legislator legislature

legitimate
reasonable; lawful
legitimacy legitimately legitimize or *legitimise*

leisure
time for relaxation

leisurely
relaxed

lemon
kind of yellow citrus fruit

lend
to give for temporary use
lent

length
measure of how long something is
lengthen lengthways lengthy

lens
curved piece of glass in optical instruments; part of the eye
lenses

leopard (fem. **leopardess**)
large member of the cat family with dark spots on a yellow skin
leopardesses

less
smaller; not so much
lessen lesser

lesson
period of instruction

let
to allow; to cause to; to allow the use of property for payment
letting

let's
(informal) let us

letter
symbol of the alphabet; written message
lettered lettering

lettuce
kind of plant with large edible green leaves

level
on a flat horizontal plane; amount; to make or become level
levelled (US *leveled*) *levelling* (US *leveling*)

liable
likely or subject (to); legally responsible
liability liabilities

liaise
to maintain contact with
liaising

liaison
communication and cooperation; love affair

liar
person who tells lies

liberal
generous; tolerant
liberality liberally

liberty
freedom from restraints or control
liberties liberate liberating liberation

library
(building or room with a) collection of books
libraries librarian

licence (US **license**)
official or legal permission; irresponsible use of freedom
licentious

license
to give a licence to; to authorize
licensee licensing

lick
to pass the tongue over

lid
cover for a box, etc.; eyelid
lidded

lie[1]
to speak falsely intending to deceive; false statement
lied lying

lie[2]
to be in a horizontal position
lain lay lying

lieutenant
military officer

life
state of being alive; period between birth and death
lives

lift
to raise; apparatus for transporting people or goods to a different level

light[1]
something that makes things visible; not dark; to ignite or illuminate
lighted or *lit lighten lighter lighting*

light[2]
having little weight; soft
lighten lighter lightest

lightning
electrical discharge between clouds or between clouds and the ground

like[1]
similar (to); in the same way as
liken likeness likewise

like[2]
to find enjoyable or agreeable
likeable or *likable liking*

likely
probable; suitable
likelier likeliest likelihood

limb
arm or leg; branch of a tree

limit
ultimate boundary; furthest degree; to restrict
limitation limited

limp[1]
to walk unevenly because of a weak leg; uneven walk

limp[2]
not firm or stiff

line[1]
narrow continuous mark made by a pen, etc.; length of cord or rope; row; route or course
linear lined liner

line[2]
to add an extra layer to the inside of a garment, etc.
lining

linen
cloth made from flax; clothes, sheets, etc., made of linen or cotton

linguist
person who speaks many foreign languages; person who studies language
linguistic linguistics

link
one of the rings or loops forming a chain; to connect
linkage

lion (fem. **lioness**)
large flesh-eating member of the cat family
lionesses

lip
fleshy edge of the mouth; edge or rim
lipped

liquefy
to make or become liquid
liquefaction liquefied liquefies liquefying

liquid
fluid; easily convertible into cash
liquidate liquidity liquidize or *liquidise*

list
series of names, words, etc., one below the other; to make a list of
listing

listen
to pay attention to; to concentrate on hearing
listener

lit
past tense and past participle of **light**[1]

literal
of the primary, explicit, or exact meaning of an expression
literalism literally

literary
of or fond of literature; formal

literate
able to read and write
literacy

literature
artistic writings; printed matter

litre (US **liter**)
metric litre of capacity, cubic decimetre

litter
rubbish, esp. when left in a public place; offspring of an animal

little
small; in a small amount
littler littlest

live[1]
to have life; to reside
living

live[2]
not dead; having power; broadcast simultaneously

lively
full of vigour or action
livelier liveliest liveliness

liver
organ that secretes bile and causes changes in the blood

living
alive or existing; means of support; benefice

load
something carried; burden or worry; to put a load on

loan
lending; something lent; to lend

lobby
entrance room; vestibule; to try to influence public officials
lobbies lobbied lobbying

local
of a particular place or district; not general
locality localities localize or *localise locally*

locate
to position; to find the situation of something
locating location

lock[1]
(to operate a) fastening mechanism for a door, gate, etc.; enclosed section of a canal where the water-level can be changed

lock[2]
strand or curl of hair

lodge
small house at the entrance to a country estate; to occupy temporarily; to fix in place
lodger lodging

log
length of tree-trunk; record of the movements of a ship or aircraft; (to record details in a) logbook
logged logging

logic
(science of) reasoning
logical logically logician

lonely
unhappy to be alone; solitary; desolate
lonelier loneliest loneliness

long[1]
not short in measurement or time

long[2]
to feel a strong or persistent desire
longing

look
to direct the eyes; to appear

loop
doubled-over piece of string, etc.; to make a loop in

loose
not confined or restrained; not compact or tight; to release or unfasten
loosely loosen loosing

lord
ruler or master; nobleman; to act in a superior manner
lordly

lorry
large motor vehicle for carrying heavy loads
lorries

lose
to mislay; to fail to keep or win
loser losing lost

loss
losing; something lost
losses

lost
unable to be found; unable to find one's way

lot
great number or quantity; fate; items for sale at an auction; plot of land

lottery
system for raising money by distributing numbered tickets some of which entitle the holder to a prize
lotteries

loud
noisy; (of colours) lurid

lounge
sitting room; to sit around lazily

love
(to feel a) strong affection or devotion; score of nil in sports, esp. tennis
lovable or *loveable lover loving*

lovely
attractive
lovelier loveliest loveliness

low
not high or tall; not loud; inferior
lower lowest

lower
(to make) less high

loyal
faithful
loyalist loyally loyalty loyalties

luck
(good) fortune; chance

lucky
enjoying good fortune; happening by chance
luckier luckiest luckily luckiness

luggage
suitcases, etc.

lump
shapeless mass; swelling; to put together, esp. indiscriminately
lumpy

lunch
(to eat a) meal in the middle of the day
luncheon

lung
one of a pair of breathing organs in the chest

luxury
something very enjoyable and pleasant but unnecessary
luxuries luxuriant luxuriate luxurious

Mm

machine
assembly of connected working parts to perform a certain task; to shape with a machine
machinery machining machinist

mad
insane or very foolish; (informal) very enthusiastic (about); very angry
madden madder maddest madly madness

madam
polite term of address to a woman

made
past tense and past participle of **make**
made-up

magazine
periodic publication; case containing cartridges for a weapon

magic
(of the) art of calling upon supernatural powers to produce wonders; conjuring tricks
magical magically magician

magistrate
officer who administers the law
magisterial magistracy or *magistrature*

magnet
body of iron, steel, etc., that attracts iron
magnetic magnetically magnetism magnetize or *magnetise*

magnificent
splendid; very fine
magnificence

magnify
to make appear larger
magnification magnified magnifier magnifies magnifying

mail
(to) post

main
principal; chief
mainly

maintain
to keep or continue; to keep in good condition; to assert
maintainable maintenance

majesty
sovereign power; title used to address a king or queen
majesties majestic majestically

major
important; of a musical scale or key; army rank; to specialize in

majority
greater or greatest part; amount by which the winning number of votes exceeds the next highest; full legal age
majorities

make
to produce, perform, or create; to cause to take place; to gain or earn; brand
made maker make-up making

male
of the sex that does not bear offspring

mall
public walkway; shopping centre

mammal
animal which suckles its young

man
human being; adult human male; to supply with people to perform a task, service, etc.
men manly manned manning mannish

manage
to be in charge of or direct; to succeed; to cope
manageability manageable management managing

manager
person in charge, esp. of a business
manageress managerial

mandate
(to give) official authorization or commission
mandating

mania
excited (violent) state; great enthusiasm (for)
maniac maniacal

manifest
clear; to show clearly; list
manifestation

manifesto
public declaration of policy
manifestos or *manifestoes*

manipulate
to handle skilfully, esp. to one's own advantage
manipulating manipulation manipulator

mankind
human beings collectively

manner
way of being, doing, speaking, etc.

manoeuvre (US **maneuver**)
carefully developed plan, esp. of troop movement; to move carefully
manoeuvrability (US *maneuverability*) *manoeuvrable* (US *maneuverable*) *manoeuvring* (US *maneuvering*)

mansion
large imposing house

manual
performed with the hands
manually

manufacture
to produce goods on a large scale, esp. with machinery; to make or invent
manufacturer manufacturing

manure
animal excrement used as fertilizer

many
large number of

map
plan or representation of part of the earth's surface; to make a detailed map or plan of
mapped mapping

marathon
long-distance running race

march
to walk with regular steps, as soldiers do; musical composition
marches

March
3rd month of the year

margarine
substitute for butter made from vegetable oils, etc.

margin
border or edge; difference between cost price and selling price; small amount
marginal marginalize or *marginalise marginally*

marine
of the sea or shipping; soldier trained for service on land or sea

mark
(to make a) visible impression on a surface; token; (to give a) figure indicating the quality of students' work
markedly

market
public place where goods are sold; to deal in or advertise a commodity
marketable marketing

marmalade
preserve made from citrus fruit, esp. oranges

marriage
state of being husband and wife; ceremony in which a man and woman become husband and wife
marriageable

marry
to join or take in marriage
married marries marrying

marsh
low soft wet land
marshy

marshal
highest-ranking military officer; official; to arrange
marshalled (US *marshaled*) *marshalling* (US *marshaling*)

marsupial
(of) a mammal that carries its young in a pouch

martial
of war

marvellous (US **marvelous**)
extraordinary; excellent
marvellously (US *marvelously*)

masculine
of men or qualities thought to be manly
masculinity

mask
(to put on a) cover worn over the face for disguise or protection

mass
large quantity; large body; to form into a mass
masses

massacre
slaughter of a great number of people or animals; to kill indiscriminately
massacres massacring

massive
large and heavy; bulky

mast
tall upright pole to support a ship's sail

master
teacher; employer; expert; skilled craftsman; to overcome; to acquire skill in or knowledge of
masterful masterly masterpiece mastery

mat
fabric used as floor covering; to tangle
matted matting

match[1]
short wooden stick with a tip that ignites by friction on a rough surface
matches

match[2]
contest; person of equal skill, etc.; to be harmonious
matches matchless

mate
breeding partner; friend; to pair for breeding
matey mating

material
substance from which a thing is made; cloth; of matter; important
materialism materialist materialistic materialize or *materialise materially*

maternal
of or like a mother; related through the mother

maternity
motherhood; (of) pregnancy

mathematics
science of numbers, quantities, etc.
mathematical mathematically mathematician

matter
physical substance; subject or material; to be of importance

mature
(to make or become) fully grown or developed; adult
maturing maturity

maximum
greatest possible (amount, etc.)
maximal maximize or *maximise*

may
auxiliary verb used to express possibility, permission, or a wish
mayn't might

May
5th month of the year

maybe
perhaps

mayor (fem. **mayoress**)
chief executive or head of a city or borough
mayoral mayoralty

me
object pronoun referring to the speaker or writer

meal
regular occasion of eating

mean[1]
not generous; poor
meanly meanness

mean[2]
to intend; to be a sign of
meant

meaning
what a word or sign represents; significance
meaningful meaningless

means
method or way; resources; income

meantime or **meanwhile**
(during the) intervening time

measure
quantity or size; standard or unit; step, action, or proposed law; to determine the size, etc., of
measurable measurement measuring

meat
flesh of animals as food
meaty

mechanic
worker skilled in using, repairing, etc., machines

mechanical
of machines
mechanically

mechanism
machinery; action
mechanistic mechanize or *mechanise*

medal
small commemorative piece of metal
medallist (US *medalist*)

media
pl. of medium

medicine
study of the prevention and cure of disease; substance used in the treatment of disease
medical medically medicate medicinal

medieval or **mediaeval**
of the Middle Ages

meditate
to think deeply
meditating meditation

medium
agency or intermediate state (pl. *media* or *mediums*); method of transmitting information (pl. *media* or *mediums*); person claiming to be an intermediary between the dead and the living
(pl. *mediums*)

meet
to come together with;
to satisfy a need or requirement
met

meeting
gathering of people for a discussion, etc.

melody
tune; pleasant sequence of sounds
melodies melodious

melt
to make or become liquid by heating
molten

member
person belonging to a club, society, etc.; part of the body
membership

memorandum
written reminder; business communication
memorandums or *memoranda*

memorial
(something) serving as a commemoration

memory
ability to remember; something remembered
memories memorabilia memorable memorably memorize or *memorise*

men
pl. of **man**

mend
to repair or rectify

mental
of or in the mind
mentally mentality

mention
brief reference; to refer to briefly
mentionable

menu
list of dishes available in a restaurant; list of options on a computer

merchant
person engaged in buying and selling goods

mercy
compassion; restraint; pity
mercies merciful merciless

mere
nothing more than
merely

merge
to unite, join, or blend
merger merging

merit
deserving quality; to deserve
merited meriting meritorious

merry
jolly; funny; (informal) slightly drunk
merrier merriest merrily merriment

mess
state of untidy confusion; place where a group of servicemen eat
messy

message
communication; to send a message to
messaging

messenger
person who takes messages

met
past tense and past participle of **meet**

metal
one of a group of mineral substances such as iron or copper; to fit or cover with metal
metalled (US *metaled*) *metallic metalling* (US *metaling*)

meteorology
study of the weather and atmosphere
meteorological meteorologist

meter
device that measures and records an amount

method
way of doing something
methodical methodology

metre (US **meter**)
basic metric unit of length; rhythmical pattern in verse
metric metrical metricate

metropolis
main city of a country
metropolises metropolitan

mice
pl. of **mouse**

microphone
device that converts sound into electrical energy

microscope
instrument with lenses that produce magnified images of tiny objects
microscopic microscopically

microwave
electromagnetic wave between 0.3 and 0.001 metres; oven in which food is cooked by microwaves; to cook in such an oven
microwaveable or *microwavable*

midday
noon

middle
(at a) point equally distant from 2 extremes
middling

midget
abnormally small person or thing

midnight
12 o'clock at night

might
past tense of **may**
mightn't

mighty
strong and powerful
mightily mightiness

migrate
to move from 1 country or area to another
migrant migrating migration

mild
gentle; moderate; not strong or extreme
mildly

mile
unit of length, 1760 yards
mileage miler

militant
aggressive (person)
militancy militantly

military
(of the) armed forces
militarily militarism militaristic

milk
whitish fluid secreted by female mammals to feed their young; to draw milk from
milky

mill
building with machinery that grinds grain into flour; factory; to grind
miller milling

millennium
period of 1000 years; time of universal happiness
millennia or *millenniums millennial*

millimetre (US **millimeter**)
1000th part of a metre

million
1,000,000
millionaire millionairess millionth

mimic
to imitate, esp. for comic effect
mimicked mimicking mimicry

mince
to chop; to moderate; minced meat
mincer mincing

mind
intellect; intelligence or understanding; to look after; to object to
mindful mindless

mine[1]
(the one or ones) belonging to me

mine[2]
excavation from which coal, etc., is dug; metal case containing explosive; to extract in a mine
miner mining

mineral
natural substance obtained by mining, etc.

miniature
small-scale; small painting, etc.
miniaturist miniaturize or *miniaturise*

minimum
lowest possible (amount, etc.)
minimal minimize or minimise

minister
government official; member of the clergy; to provide help (to)
ministerial ministration

ministry
government department; duties of the clergy
ministries

minor
less; of a musical scale or key; person not legally of age

minority
smaller or smallest part; period when a person is under legal age
minorities

minuscule
extremely small

minute[1]
one-sixtieth of an hour or a degree

minute[2]
tiny
minutely

miracle
extraordinary event, esp. with a supernatural cause
miraculous miraculously

mirror
piece of glass that reflects images; to reflect
mirrored mirroring

misbehave
to behave badly
misbehaving misbehaviour (US *misbehavior*)

miscellaneous
of a variety of kinds
miscellany miscellanies

mischief
foolish or playful behaviour, esp. by children
mischievous

miserable
very unhappy
miserably

misery
great unhappiness
miseries

misfortune
bad luck

mislay
to lose temporarily
mislaid mislaying

mislead
to lead in a wrong direction; to give false information to
misleading misled

miss
to fail to hit, catch, achieve, etc.; to discover or regret the absence of; failure to hit, etc.
misses missed missing

Miss
title of an unmarried girl or woman
Misses

missile
thrown or projected object or weapon

mission
group of envoys; task, duty, or vocation
missionary missionaries

misspell
to spell wrongly
misspelled or misspelt *misspelling*

mist
(to cover with a) thin fog
misty

mistake
error; to misunderstand or confuse
mistaken mistakenly mistaking mistook

mistress
woman in authoritative position; woman teacher; man's lover
mistresses

misunderstand
to understand wrongly
misunderstanding misunderstood

mix
to combine or blend; to be sociable; something mixed
mixes mixer mixture

mnemonic
aid to one's memory

moan
(to utter a) low mournful sound; to grumble

mob
disorderly crowd; to attack or acclaim in a large crowd
mobbed mobbing

mobile
easily movable; small portable telephone; hanging structure with moving parts
mobility

mock
to ridicule; sham or imitation
mockery mockeries

mode
manner or way something is done; fashion

model
small-scale representation; pattern; person who wears clothes to display them; exemplary; to shape
modelled (US *modeled*) *modeller* (US *modeler*) *modelling* (US *modeling*)

moderate
not extreme or excessive; to make moderate
moderating moderation

modern
of the present time
modernity modernize or *modernise*

modest
not vain or boastful; small or unpretentious
modesty

modify
to adapt, change, or qualify
modification modified modifies modifying

module
standard unit in measurement; independent component or unit
modular

moist
slightly wet
moisten moistness moisture

mole[1]
small dark pigment on human skin

mole[2]
kind of small burrowing mammal

molecule
smallest particle of a substance that still retains its chemical properties
molecular

moment
very short time; importance
momentary momentous

monarch
king or queen
monarchic monarchism monarchist monarchy monarchies

Monday
2nd day of the week

money
coins and banknotes; wealth
moneys or *monies moneyed*

monitor
senior pupil; device that checks or controls; screen; to check

monkey
long-tailed primate
monkeys

monopoly
(person or group having) exclusive control of something
monopolies monopolize or *monopolise*

monster
imaginary beast; wicked person
monstrosity monstrosities monstrous

month
1 of 12 divisions of the year
monthly monthlies

monument
thing built to commemorate a person or event
monumental monumentally

mood
state of mind or spirit
moody

moon
natural satellite of the earth

moonlight
light from the moon; to have two paid jobs
moonlighting moonlit

moor[1]
expanse of open land, esp. covered with gorse or heather

moor[2]
to secure a vessel with a rope or cable
mooring

moral
concerned with right and wrong; moral lesson or principle
moralist moralistic morality moralities moralize or moralise

morale
confidence of a group

more
(to a) greater number, degree, etc.; additional
moreish

moreover
in addition

morning
period of the day until noon

mortal
subject to death; causing death; human being
mortality mortally

mortgage
(to give a) claim on property as security for payment of a loan
mortgagee mortgaging mortgagor

mosque
Muslim place of worship

mosquito
kind of insect, the female of which sucks blood
mosquitoes

most
(to the) greatest number, degree, etc.
mostly

mother
female parent; woman leader of a convent; to give birth to or look after in a motherly way
motherhood mother-in-law mothers-in-law motherliness motherly

motion
movement; proposal suggested to a meeting; to signal by gesturing
motionless

motivate
to give an incentive to; to inspire
motivating motivation

motive
incentive; reason; causing motion

motor
engine that causes motion; motor car; to drive
motorist

motorway
special road for fast travel

mould[1] (US **mold**)
shaped hollow used to give a definite form to something; to give shape or form to
moulding (US *molding*)

mould[2] (US **mold**)
fungus that forms on damp or decaying matter
mouldy (US *moldy*)

mount
mountain; support; to climb; to increase; to climb up on; to initiate

mountain
high landmass
mountaineer mountaineering mountainous

mourn
to feel or express sorrow over the death of someone or a loss
mourner mournful mourning

mouse
small long-tailed rodent; small cursor-moving device attached to a computer
mice mousy

moustache (US **mustache**)
hair that is allowed to grow on the upper lip

mouth
opening through which food is taken into the body; opening or outlet
mouthful

move
to change position; to proceed; to arouse an emotion in; to propose
movable or moveable moving

movement
change of position; group of people with a common purpose

Mr
title of a man, whether married or unmarried

Mrs
title of a married woman

Ms
title of a woman, whether married or unmarried

much
(to a) great extent or amount

mud
soft wet earth or clay

muddle
to mix or confuse; confusion
muddling

muddy
covered with mud; to make or become muddy
muddied muddier muddies muddiest muddiness muddying

mug
drinking container with a handle; to attack and rob
mugged mugger mugging

multiple
having many parts; quantity that contains another quantity an exact number of times

multiply
to add a quantity to itself a given number of times
multiplication multiplicity multiplied multiplier multiplies multiplying

mum
(informal) mother

mumble
to utter unclearly; unclear utterance
mumbling

mummy[1]
(informal) mother
mummies

mummy[2]
preserved embalmed body
mummies mummify

municipal
of a town, city, borough or its local government
municipality municipalities municipally

murder
killing of another person with intent; to kill in this way
murderer murderess murderous

murmur
(to make a) low indistinct sound

muscle
tissue of elongated cells that expand and contract
muscular muscularity

museum
where interesting objects are exhibited

mushroom
fungus with a slender stalk and cap

music
art of combining and ordering sounds
musical musicality musically musician

must
auxiliary verb to express obligation, etc.
mustn't

mutter
to utter in a low unclear way; such an utterance

mutual
felt or directed by each towards or to the other
mutuality mutually

my
possessive form of **I**

myself
reflexive form of **I**

mystery
thing that cannot be or has not been explained
mysteries mysterious mysteriously

myth
traditional fictitious story; something imaginary
mythical mythological mythology mythologies

Nn

nail
horny layer at the end of fingers or toes; (to join with a) small thin metal spike

naive or **naïve**
unsophisticated; innocent; artless
naively or *naïvely*
naïveté or *naïvety*

naked
wearing no clothes

name
word by which a person or thing is known or identified; reputation; to give a name to
nameless namely naming

nappy
piece of cloth or paper worn by babies to absorb their excrement
nappies

narrate
to tell a story
narrating narration narrative narrator

narrow
(to make or become) small in breadth
narrowly narrowness

nasty
unpleasant; mean or spiteful
nastier nastiest nastily nastiness

nation
people living in the same country or under the same government

national
of a nation; citizen
nationalism nationalist nationality nationalities nationalize or *nationalise*

native
person born in a particular place; belonging to a particular place

natural
of nature; not artificial; simple
naturally

nature
set of essential qualities; system of existence and forces; plants and animals
naturalism naturalist naturalistic

naughty
mischievous; disobedient
naughtier naughtiest naughtily naughtiness

naval
of a navy

navel
small depression in the middle of the abdomen

navy
country's warships; branch of the armed services comprising such ships
navies

near
(to come or go) close to
nearby

nearly
almost

neat
tidy and clean
neaten

necessary
(something) essential
necessaries necessarily

necessity
necessary thing; need
necessities necessitate necessitating

neck
part of an animal connecting the head to the rest of the body

necklace
decorative object, consisting of jewels, etc., on a chain or string, worn round the neck

need
to require; to be necessary; reason; distress
needful needless needn't needy

needle
thin pointed piece of metal used in sewing or knitting; to irritate
needling

negative
indicating a refusal or denial; type of electric charge; photographic image with the positive dark and light parts reversed; less than zero
negatively negativity

neglect
to fail to look after; to omit to do something
neglectful negligence negligent negligible

negotiate
to discuss in order to reach an agreement
negotiable negotiating negotiation negotiator

neighbour (US **neighbor**)
person who lives near to another
neighbourhood (US *neighborhood*) *neighbouring* (US *neighboring*) *neighbourliness* (US *neighborliness*) *neighbourly* (US *neighborly*)

neither
not 1 nor the other (of 2); not either; nor

nephew
son of one's sister or brother

nerve
fibre that transmits impulses between part of the body and a nerve-centre; courage; (informal) impudence
nervy

nervous
of the nerves; anxious

nest
structure in which birds rear their young

net[1]
(to cover with an) openwork fabric of string, wire, etc.; to catch in a net
netted netting

net[2] or **nett**
remaining after all deductions have been made; to gain by profit
netted netting

network
system of crossing lines; interconnected system
networking

neutral
not belonging to either side in a war; with no special features; gear that does not allow either forward or backward movement in a vehicle
neutrality neutralize or *neutralise*

never
at no time

nevertheless
despite this

new
recently made; additional
newly

news
description of recent interesting events
newsworthy newsy

newspaper
daily, weekly, etc., publication providing news

next
following immediately; closest

nice
pleasant; fine
nicely niceness nicer nicest nicety niceties

niche
recess in a wall for a vase, etc.; specially suitable job, etc.

niece
daughter of one's sister or brother

night
period of darkness between sunset and sunrise
nightie

nightmare
frightening dream
nightmarish

nil
nothing

nine
number 9
ninth

nineteen
number 19
nineteenth

ninety
number 90
nineties ninetieth

nitrogen
colourless odourless gas present in the air

no
used to deny, refuse, etc.; not any
noes

noble
aristocratic; honourable
nobility nobler noblest nobly

nobody
no one; insignificant person
nobodies

nod
to move the head down and up to show agreement, etc.
nodded nodding

noise
sound, esp. a harsh and loud one
noiseless noisier noisiest noisily noisiness noisy

none
not any; not at all; to no extent

nonsense
something that is unintelligible, meaningless, or absurd
nonsensical

noon
12 o'clock midday

no one or **no-one**
nobody

nor
and not

normal
usual or ordinary
normality normalize or *normalise normally*

north
one of the 4 compass points, opposite of south
north-east or *northeast northerly northern northerner northward northwards north-west* or *northwest*

nose
organ of smell and breathing; sense of smell; front end; to find out by smelling
nosing

nosey or **nosy**
(informal) inquisitive
nosier nosiest nosily nosiness

not
used to express negation

notable
distinguished; remarkable
notability notabilities notably

note
(to write a) brief comment; to notice; musical sound
noting

notebook
small book in which to make *notes*

nothing
not anything
nothingness

notice
to become aware of; public announcement; attention; warning
noticeable noticeably

notify
to inform or announce
notifiable notification notified notifies notifying

notion
concept, idea, or whim
notional

notorious
well-known for being bad
notoriety

nought
zero

noun
word referring to a person, place, or thing

novel[1]
long work of narrative fiction
novelette novelist

novel[2]
new; original
novelty novelties

November
11th month of the year

now
at the present time

nowadays
in this present period

nowhere
not anywhere

nuclear
of a nucleus or the power or energy it contains

nucleus
central part; positively charged core of an atom
nuclei

nude
naked
nudism nudist nudity

nuisance
annoying person or thing

numb
deprived of sense or feeling; to make numb
numbness

number
symbol used in counting; to count

numerous
many; great in number

nurse
person skilled in looking after the ill or young children; to look after; to suckle
nursing

nursery
place where young children are looked after; playroom; place where young plants are grown
nurseries

nut
dry fruit or seed with a hard shell and an edible kernel; piece of metal used with a bolt to fasten or tighten
nutty

nylon
synthetic fibre

Oo

oak
tree of the beech family producing acorns

oar
pole with a blade used to propel and steer a boat

oath
solemn vow; curse

obedient
willing to do as one is told
obedience

obese
very fat
obesity

obey
to do as one is told; to comply with rules

object[1]
solid thing; purpose or aim; (grammar) noun, etc., that is acted on by a verb

object[2]
to argue against
objection objectionable objector

objective
independent; purpose or aim
objectivity

obligation
something one is bound to do
obligate obligating

oblige
to require by law; to help
obliging

obliterate
to wipe out
obliterating obliteration

oblong
4-sided (figure) with adjacent sides unequal

obnoxious
very unpleasant

obscene
offensive; indecent
obscenity

obscure
(to make) unclear or dim; not well known
obscuring obscurity

observe
to watch; to conform to; to commemorate; to remark
observance observant observation observatory observatories observer observing

obsess
to preoccupy the mind
obsesses obsession obsessive

obsolete
out of date
obsolescence obsolescent

obstacle
hindrance to progress

obstinate
holding firmly to an opinion
obstinacy

obstruct
to block with an obstacle
obstruction obstructive

obtain
to acquire; (formal) to be in existence
obtainable

obvious
very clear or evident
obviously

occasion
time or opportunity; reason

occasional
happening from time to time
occasionally

occupation
occupying; job or profession
occupational

occupy
to stay in; to take up; to keep busy
occupancy occupant occupied occupier occupies occupying

occur
to happen; to come to mind
occurred occurrence occurring

ocean
one of the earth's 5 great seas
oceanic oceanography

o'clock
used to show the hour of the day or night

October
10th month of the year

octopus
sea animal with 8 tentacles
octopuses or *octopi*

odd
unusual or peculiar; not even; incidental
oddity oddities oddly

odds
probability, sometimes expressed as a ratio

of
belonging to; containing; concerning; from; made from

off
away; not on; completed

offence (US **offense**)
breaking of a law

offend
to break a law; to insult

offensive
unpleasant; rude; attack

offer
to present; to be willing; something offered
offered offering

office
room where business is carried on; position of authority or responsibility

officer
holder of a position of authority or responsibility

official
person who holds an office; of an office; authorized

officiate
to be officially in charge (at)
officiating

offspring
children or young of animals

often
frequently

oil
smooth greasy liquid; petroleum; to lubricate
oily

OK
expression of approval; to approve
OK's OK'd OK'ing

old
aged; known for a long time; former
olden older oldest

old-fashioned
out of date

omelette (US **omelet**)
dish made of beaten eggs

omen
sign of something good or evil in the future

ominous
threatening

omit
to leave out; to neglect
omission omitted omitting

on
touching or attached to; covering; supported by; concerning; operating

once
one time; in the past

one
number 1; individual; people generally

oneself
reflexive form of one

onion
kind of plant grown for its rounded bulb

online
connected to the Internet

only
single; merely; exclusive(ly); however

onto
so as to be on the surface or top of; in addition to

open
not closed; to make or become open; to begin
opener openly openness

opening
gap or hole; opportunity; (occurring at the) beginning

opera
dramatic production set to music
operatic operetta

operate
to work or function; to perform surgery
operable operating operative operator

operation
operating; surgical procedure; series of actions carried out to achieve a purpose
operational

opinion
judgement or view
opinionated

opponent
someone who opposes; person one fights or plays against

opportunity
favourable chance or circumstance
opportunities opportune opportunist

oppose
to fight against
opposing opposition

opposite
facing; contrary; corresponding

oppress
to rule over unjustly
oppresses oppression oppressive oppressor

opt
to choose

optimism
inclination to expect the best
optimist optimistic optimistically

option
choice; thing chosen

optional
left to individual choice

or
used in front of an alternative

oral
spoken; verbal; of or through the mouth; type of spoken exam
orally

orange
kind of round juicy citrus fruit; yellowish-red

orchestra
large group of musicians playing different instruments
orchestral orchestrate orchestration

order
manner in which things are arranged; request to supply goods; to arrange; to command; to request goods
orderly

ordinary
usual; familiar; commonplace; unexceptional
ordinarily ordinariness

organ
musical keyboard instrument with pipes; part of the body with a particular function
organist

organic
of bodily organs or living organisms; grown without using chemical fertilizers, etc.
organically

organization or **organisation**
group of people working together for a particular purpose; arranging or organizing
organizational or *organisational*

organize or **organise**
to arrange systematically
organizing or *organising*

origin
source or beginning

original
first; (being the) source
originality originally

ornament
thing that adds decoration or enhances the appearance; to decorate
ornamental ornamentation

orthodox
of generally established views
orthodoxy

oscillate
to swing to and fro; to move between extremes
oscillating oscillation

other
remaining; different

otherwise
alternatively; differently

ought
auxiliary verb used to express obligation, etc.
oughtn't

ounce
unit of weight, one sixteenth of a pound

our
possessive form of we

ours
(the one or ones) belonging to us

ourselves
reflexive form of we

out
away from; not alight; revealed; exhausted

outbreak
sudden appearance or occurrence

outcome
consequence or result

outdoor
(taking place) in the open air
outdoors

outer
external

outfit
set of clothing or equipment for a particular task

outing
trip or journey for pleasure

outlet
vent or opening; place where something is sold

outline
(to draw a) line surrounding the edge of something; (to present a) preliminary plan or summary
outlining

outlook
(point of) view; prospects for the future

output
amount produced; production; to produce
outputting

outrage
offensive or violent act; great shock; to shock greatly
outraging outrageous

outright
absolute; absolutely

outside
(at or to the) exterior

outskirts
outlying areas of a city

outstanding
excellent; unresolved or unpaid
outstandingly

oven
enclosed compartment in which food is baked or roasted

over
above; more than; across; remaining
overly overmuch

overall
including everything; (or overalls) loose-fitting protective garment

overboard
over the side of a boat or ship and into the water**overcome**
to defeat; to succeed in dealing with
overcame overcoming

overdraft
amount owed to the bank by the holder of a bank account

overflow
to flow over the limits of
overflowing

overhang
to extend over
overhung

overlap
to cover or coincide partly
overlapped overlapping

overlook
to have as a view from above; to fail to see

overnight
during or for the night

overseas
across the seas; abroad

overtake
to move past another vehicle by travelling faster; to come upon suddenly
overtaken overtook overtaking

overthrow
to defeat; to upset
overthrew overthrown

overtime
(work undertaken) in addition to normal hours

overwhelm
to engulf or overcome

owe
to be in debt to
owing

owl
nocturnal bird of prey

own
individual; to possess; to acknowledge
owner ownership

ox
kind of bovine mammal; adult castrated male of species of cattle
oxen

oxygen
colourless odourless gas

oyster
kind of edible shellfish

ozone
form of oxygen; pure sea air

Pp

pace
single walking step;
speed or rate; to walk slowly
pacing

pack
(to put into a) container or bundle; group of dogs or wolves; set of playing-cards;
to crowd or fill

package
(to put in a) parcel; number of items or services offered together
packaging

packet
(to wrap up in a) small pack
packeted packeting

pact
agreement or alliance

pad
(to fill with a) soft cushioning material; set of blank paper; launching area for helicopter or spacecraft
padded padding

paddle
(to propel a boat with a) short oar; to walk about barefoot in shallow water
paddling

paedophilia
(US **pedophilia**)
sexual desire towards children
paedophile (US *pedophile*)

page[1]
leaf of paper in a book;
one side of this

page[2]
young boy-servant; to summon by name over a public-address system
pager paging

pageant
colourful public display
pageantry

paid
past tense and past participle of pay

pain
bodily suffering; anguish in the mind
painful painless

paint
(to cover with a) liquid colouring substance
painter painting

pair
set of 2 things that go together;
to put together in pairs

palace
official residence of a monarch or high official such as a president
palatial

pale
lacking brightness or intensity

palette
thin board used by artists for mixing colours

pallet
portable platform used for storing and transporting goods

palm[1]
inner part of the hand

palm[2]
kind of tropical tree or shrub

pamphlet
leaflet or booklet
pamphleteer

pan
round shallow cooking vessel; to wash earth while searching for gold
panned panning

pane
sheet of glass in a window

panel
(to provide with a) flat section of a surface; group of people, esp. jury; board of controls
panelled (US *paneled*) *panelling* (US *paneling*) *panellist* (US *panelist*)

panic
(to feel) sudden uncontrollable fear
panicked panicking panicky

panorama
wide scenic view; survey
panoramic panoramically

pant
to breathe in short quick bursts

pants
underpants; knickers; (US) trousers

paper
substance made from pulped wood, etc., used for writing on

par
average or standard; standard score for each hole on a golf-course
parity

parachute
device that slows down the speed of fall from a great height; to descend by parachute
parachuting parachutist

parade
ordered march or assembly of troops; (to march in) procession; row of shops
parading

paradise
blissful place

paragraph
division of a piece of writing

parallel
constantly at the same distance from each other and never meeting; corresponding; to be similar or equal to
paralleled paralleling parallelogram

paralyse (US **paralyze**)
to cause to lose the ability to move or feel
paralysing (US *paralyzing*) *paralysis paralytic*

parasite
animal, plant, or person living off another
parasitic

parcel
(to wrap up in a) package
parcelled (US *parceled*) *parcelling* (US *parceling*)

pardon
to excuse or forgive a mistake or offence; forgiveness
pardonable pardonably

parent
father or mother
parentage parental parentally parenthood parenting

parish
district with its own church
parishes parishioner parochial

park
open land for recreation; to stop and leave a vehicle temporarily in a place
parking

parliament
(representatives in the) law-making assembly of a country
parliamentarian parliamentary

parrot
bird with bright plumage and the ability to mimic sounds

part
piece, portion, or subdivision; to divide

partial
not total; not fair; fond of
partiality partially

participate
to take part in
participant participating participation participator participatory

participle
verbal form usually ending in -ing or -ed

particle
very small piece or amount

particular
individual; special
particularity particularize or *particularise particularly*

partly
not wholly; in part

partner
person someone lives, works, or plays with; to be a partner to
partnership

party
social gathering; organized political group
parties

pass
to move onwards or proceed by; to hand over; to be accepted or successful; written permission; narrow gap in mountains
passes passable passer-by passing

passage
passing; corridor; brief section of a book, etc.

passenger
person travelling in a vehicle

passion
deep feeling, esp. love
passionate passionately

passive
acted on by external forces; not resisting
passivity

passport
official nationality and identity document carried by travellers abroad

past
(belonging to an) earlier time; no longer existing; after; beyond

pasta
flour and water dough preparation; spaghetti, macaroni, lasagne, etc.

paste
soft mixture; (to stick with an) adhesive
pasting pasty

pasteurize or **pasteurise**
to sterilize by heating briefly
pasteurization or *pasteurisation*
pasteurizing or *pasteurising*

pastry
dough of flour, fat, and water, esp. baked
pastries

pat
to tap softly with the hand; small lump of butter
patted patting

patch
(to cover with a) piece of material for mending
patches patchwork patchy

paternal
of or like a father; related through the father

path
track or way

pathetic
arousing pity or sympathy; (informal) miserably inadequate
pathetically pathos

patience
being tolerant and calm; card-game for 1 person

patient
tolerant and calm; person receiving medical care

patrol
to go around an area to maintain security; security check of area; group patrolling an area
patrolled patrolling

patron (fem. **patroness**)
person who supports a good cause; regular customer
patronage

patronize or **patronise**
to act as a patron; to behave condescendingly towards
patronizing or *patronising*

patter
to tap quickly and repeatedly; tapping noise; sales talk

pattern
repeated, esp. decorative design; model; to arrange with a pattern

pause
(to take a) temporary rest
pausing

pave
to cover with a firm surface, esp. using flat stones or concrete
pavement paving

paw
clawed foot of an animal

pay
to give money in return for goods or services; salary or wages
paid payable payee payer *paying payment*

pea
edible green seed of climbing plant

peace
ending or absence of war; calm
peaceable peaceably peaceful peacefully peacemaker peacetime

peach
juicy stoned fruit with a reddish-yellow skin
peaches peachy

peak
sharp top of a mountain; projecting edge of a cap

pear
kind of fleshy rounded fruit that narrows towards the stalk
pear-shaped

pearl
hard round mass found in an oyster and valued as a gem
pearly

peasant
small landowner or farm labourer
peasantry

peculiar
odd; special; exclusive (to)
peculiarity peculiarities peculiarly

pedal
(to operate by a) lever for the foot
pedalled (US *pedaled*) *pedalling* (US *pedaling*)

peddle
to go from place to place selling goods; to sell drugs
peddler peddling pedlar

pedestrian
person walking on foot; dull
pedestrianize or *pedestrianise*

peek
to glance quickly; quick glance

peel
(to remove the) skin or rind
peeler peeling

peep
to look through an opening or from a hidden place; quick look
peep peeping

peer[1] (fem. **peeress**)
member of British nobility; someone's equal
peeresses peerage peerless

peer[2]
to look at intently

peg
(to fasten with a) small clip or pin
pegged pegging

pen[1]
instrument for writing or drawing with ink; to write or draw with a pen
penned penning

pen[2]
(to confine in a) small enclosure
penned penning

a b c d e f g h i j k l m n o p q r s t u v w x y z

penalty
punishment; (soccer) kick at goal from close range
penalties penalize or penalise

pence
pl. of **penny**

pencil
(to write or draw with an) implement containing a strip of graphite
pencilled (US *penciled*) *pencilling* (US *penciling*)

penetrate
to pass through or into
penetrable penetrating penetration penetrative

penguin
flightless short-legged sea bird

penicillin
antibiotic obtained from a mould

penny
bronze coin, 100 of which are worth £1 sterling
pence or *pennies penniless*

pension
regular fixed sum of money paid to older people, etc.
pensionable pensioner

people
human beings; nation or tribe; to populate
people peopling

pepper
sharp hot powder for sprinkling on food; green, red, or yellow fruit; to sprinkle pepper over
peppered peppering peppery

per
for every; according to

perceive
to become aware of
perceivable perceiving

per
cent in each hundred
percentage

perception
awareness or observation
perceptible perceptibly perceptive

perch
place on which a bird rests; (esp. of a bird) to rest
perches

perennial
(of a plant) growing for several years; never ending or changing

perfect
faultless; complete; to make perfect
perfectible perfection perfectionism perfectionist perfectly

perform
to carry out; to act a part
performance performer

perfume
preparation of fragrant oils, etc.; sweet pleasant smell; to impart a perfume to
perfumer perfumery perfumeries perfuming

perhaps
possibly

period
portion or interval of time; school lesson; occurrence of menstruation
periodic periodically

periodical
magazine published regularly

perish
to be destroyed; to die;
to decay
perishability perishable perishes perishing

perk[1]
incidental benefit; bonus

perk[2]
to liven (up)
perky

permanent
lasting indefinitely;
not expected to change
permanence permanently

permission
act of allowing someone
to do something
permissible permissive

permit
to allow; to consent to; document giving permission
permitted permitting

perpetual
never-ending
perpetually perpetuate perpetuity

perplex
to confuse or complicate
perplexes perplexity

persecute
to harass or cause to suffer
persecuting persecution persecutor

persevere
to continue steadily and not give up
perseverance persevering

persist
to carry on in spite of difficulties
or objections;
to continue
persistence persistent

person
human being
people or *persons*

personal
of a person; belonging to oneself;
private
personalize or *personalise personally*

personality
sum of individual characteristics
of a person; well-known person
personalities

personnel
employees in an organization

perspective
art of drawing 3 dimensions on a 2-dimensional surface; way of looking at different problems and giving them relative importance

persuade
to urge successfully,
esp. by reasoning; to convince
persuadable persuading persuasion persuasive

pessimism
inclination to expect the worst
pessimist pessimistic pessimistically

pest
annoying person or thing

pester
to annoy constantly

pet
domesticated animal; favourite; to pamper; to fondle
petted petting

petal
leaf-like part of flower head
petalled (US *petaled*)

petition
(to make a) formal appeal or request, esp. one signed by many people
petitioner

petrol
refined petroleum used as fuel

petticoat
woman's underskirt

petty
trivial; unimportant; small-minded
pettier pettiest pettily pettiness

pharmacy
(shop) preparing or dispensing drugs
pharmacies pharmaceutical pharmacist pharmacology

phase
stage in a sequence or development; to make happen in stages
phasing

phenomenon
observable fact or event; significant person or thing
phenomena phenomenal phenomenally

philosophy
study of existence, truth, etc., and right behaviour; system of beliefs
philosophies philosopher philosophical philosophically philosophize or *philosophise*

phone
(to use the) telephone
phoning

phoney or **phony**
(informal) false
phonier phoniest phonily phoniness

photo
short for photograph
photos

photocopy
(to make a) photographic copy of a document, etc.
photocopies photocopied photocopier photocopying

photograph
image recorded by a camera
photographer photographic photographically photography

phrase
group of words; expression; to express in a phrase
phrasal phraseology phrasing

physical
of the body; of material things
physically

physics
science concerned with matter and energy
physicist

physique
person's general physical form and structure

piano
musical keyboard instrument; (music) softly
pianos pianist

pick[1]
to choose or select; to gather fruit

pick[2]
pointed tool for breaking rocks
or hard ground
pickaxe (US *pickax*)

picnic
(to take part in an) outing
with an informal meal in the open air
picnicked *picnicker* picnicking

picture
painting or representation; mental
image; to describe or imagine
pictorial picturing

picturesque
pleasant; charming

pie
baked dish of meat, fruit, etc.,
in pastry

piece
part of; fragment; esp. musical
composition; coin; to join (together)
piecing

pier
structure extending into the sea;
support for an arch or bridge

pierce
to make a hole in something,
esp. with a sharp instrument

pig
stout-bodied mammal with a long
blunt snout; (informal) greedy or
unpleasant person
piggery piggeries piggish piggy
piggies piglet

pigeon
bird of the dove family

pile
heap; nuclear reactor; raised surface
on a fabric; to gather into a pile
piling

pill
small tablet of medicine;
oral contraceptive

pillar
upright structure

pillow
supporting cushion for
the head

pilot
person qualified to control an aircraft
or to guide a ship; to act as a pilot;
trial or experimental (broadcast)
piloted piloting

pin
(to fasten with a) short pointed piece
of metal
pinned pinning

pinch
to squeeze tightly between finger and
thumb; such a squeeze;
(informal) to steal
pinches

pine[1]
kind of evergreen tree

pine[2]
to long for
pining

pink
pale red colour; kind of garden plant;
very good condition

pint
measure of liquid capacity, one-eighth of a gallon

pioneer
explorer of new land; person who does something first; to be a pioneer
pioneered pioneering

pipe
tube for gas or liquid to flow through; (to play a) wind instrument; object in which tobacco is smoked
piper piping

pirate
sea robber; to use, copy, etc., illegally
piracy piratical pirating

pirouette
(to perform a) rapid dancing spin
pirouetting

pistol
handgun

pit
hole in the ground; to mark with dents or hollows
pitted pitting

pitch
to throw; to set up a tent or camp; playing area for sport
pitches

pity
(to feel) sympathy and sorrow for another's suffering
pities piteous pitied pitiful pitiless pitying

pizza
baked Italian dish of dough covered with cheese, tomatoes, etc.
pizzas pizzeria

placard
(to advertise by a) poster

place
(to set in a) particular point within an area, or a surface, or in space
placement placing

plaice
kind of flatfish

plain
simple; undecorated; clear or obvious; frank; not good-looking; flat area of ground
plainly plainness

plan
detailed scheme or method; drawing of a building; to make a plan
planned planner planning

plane[1]
aircraft; level (surface); (to level with a) levelling tool having a sharp metal blade
planing

plane[2]
kind of tall tree having leaves with pointed lobes

planet
heavenly body that revolves around the sun
planetarium planetariums

plank
long thin piece of wood

plant
living organism that grows with roots in the ground; machinery and equipment; factory; to set in the soil to grow
plantation

plaster
(to coat with a) mixture of lime, sand, and water applied to walls; adhesive bandage
plasterer

plastic
(made of a) synthetic substance that can be moulded
plasticity

plate
shallow dish for food; (to cover with a) coating, as of metal or glass
plating

platform
flat raised structure or floor

play
(to take part in a) game or recreation; to perform on a musical instrument; dramatic work performed on stage
player playful playing

playground
area for children to play in

playwright
dramatist

plea
earnest appeal; argument presented by a lawyer

plead
to request or try to persuade earnestly; to make a plea in a law-court
pleaded or *pled pleading*

pleasant
agreeable or friendly
pleasantly pleasantry pleasantries

please
to bring satisfaction to; used to express polite requests
pleased pleasing pleasingly

pleasure
enjoyment; satisfaction
pleasurable pleasurably

pledge
(to give a) solemn promise; (to give as a) security
pledging

plenty
abundance; enough
plentiful plentifully

pliable
easily moulded or influenced
pliability pliancy pliant

plight
predicament

plod
to walk with slow heavy steps; to work steadily
plodded plodder plodding

plot
small piece of ground; story-line in a drama, etc.; (to plan a) conspiracy; (to make a) plan
plotted plotter plotting

plough (US **plow**)
(to use an) implement with sharp blades to cut and turn over soil

pluck
to pull the feathers off; to pull out; courage
plucky

plug
stopper; device that makes electrical connections; to block with a plug
plugged plugging

plum
kind of (tree that bears a) fleshy sweet fruit; (informal) very desirable

plumb
lead weight used to measure the depth of water or to check that something is vertical

plumber
person who installs and repairs pipes and fixtures for water and drainage
plumbing

plump[1]
chubby; rounded

plump[2]
to drop heavily; (informal) to opt (for)

plunder
to rob or steal, esp. in wartime; looted goods; looting

plunge
to dive into; to thrust into
plunger plunging

plural
(grammar) referring to more than one person or thing
plurality pluralize or *pluralise*

plus
with the addition of; bonus or advantage
pluses or *plusses*

ply
to work at; to journey (between); to supply constantly (with)
plied plies plying

pneumatic
operated by compressed air
pneumatically

poach[1]
to cook in a simmering liquid

poach[2]
to take game illegally while trespassing

pocket
(to put into a) small bag sewn into a garment
pocketed pocketing

poem
verse composition
poet poetic poetical poetically poetry

point
dot; position; sharp tip; aim; to direct or indicate
pointed pointer pointless

poison
(to give a) deadly substance
poisoner poisonous

poke
to thrust or jab
poker poking

pole[1]
long thin rounded piece of wood or metal

pole[2]
either of the ends of the earth's axis; either of the terminals of an electric cell
polar polarity polarize or *polarise*

police
civil force with the duty of maintaining public order; to control
policeman policing

policy
course of action; document setting out insurance contract
policies

polish
(substance used) to make smooth and shiny by rubbing
polishes polisher

polite
well-mannered; courteous
politely politeness politer politest

politics
study or art of government
political politically politician politicize or *politicise*

poll
casting of votes in an election; survey of public opinion; to vote

pollute
to make dirty; to contaminate
pollutant polluting pollution

polythene
light plastic material

pond
pool of still water

ponder
to think about deeply

pony
small horse
ponies

pool
small area of still water; (to put into a) communal fund
pooled pooling

poor
having little money; unsatisfactory
poorly

pop[1]
(to cause to make an) explosive sound
popped popper popping

pop[2]
popular music

popular
commonly liked; of the people
popularity popularize or *popularise popularly*

populate
to inhabit an area
populace populating population populous

pore[1]
small opening, esp. in the skin
porosity porous

pore[2] (**pore over**)
to study closely
pouring

pork
flesh of pigs used as food

port
(town or city with a) harbour; left side of a ship or aircraft when facing forward

portable
able to be carried easily
portability

portfolio
flat case for holding drawings, etc.; investor's securities; duties of a government minister
portfolios

portion
part or bit; helping of food; to divide

portrait
picture or description of a person
portraitist portraiture

portray
to make a portrait; to describe
portrayal portrayed portraying

pose
(to place in a) particular position; to pretend
poser poseur posing

position
(to put in a) particular place
positional

positive
definite; explicit; absolute; type of electric charge; photographic image; greater than zero
positively positivity

possess
to own; to take control of
possesses possession possessive possessor

possible
capable of existing or being done
possibility possibilities possibly

post[1]
length of wood, metal, etc., fixed into the ground; to fasten a notice to a board, etc.

post[2]
place where a soldier is stationed; job or office; to station or appoint

post[3]
(system for delivering) letters and parcels; to send by post
postage postal

postcard
piece of card for sending a message by post

poster
placard or large notice

postman (fem. **postwoman**)
person whose job is to deliver letters and parcels
postmen postwomen

postpone
to delay until later
postponement postponing

pot
rounded container used esp. for cooking; (slang) cannabis; to put in a pot; to shorten
potted potting

potato
plant grown for its edible tubers
potatoes

potential
possible but not yet realized
potentiality potentially

poultry
domesticated birds kept for eggs or meat
poulterer

pound[1]
unit of weight, 16 ounces; unity of money in the UK and various other countries

pound[2]
to crush; to hit heavily and loudly

pour
to (cause to) flow

poverty
state of being pour

powder
fine loose dry particles; to cover with or reduce to powder
powdery

power
ability to do something; force or authority; esp. electrical energy; to supply power to

powerful
possessing great strength or force
powerfully

practicable
capable of being carried out
practicability

practical
of action; not theoretical; sensible; skilled at doing or making things
practicality practicalities

practice
regular repeated exercise; method or habit; professional business of lawyer or doctor
practician practitioner

practise (US **practice**)
to carry out; to perform regularly to develop one's skill
practising (US *practicing*)

praise
to express a favourable opinion of; to extol God
praiseworthy praising

pray
to speak to God; to entreat
prayed praying

prayer
request or communication made to God

preach
to deliver a sermon
preaches

precede
to go, come, or occur before
precedence precedent preceding

precious
loved; valuable; very fussy
preciousness preciosity

precipice
very steep rock face
precipitate precipitous

precise
exact; accurate; careful
precisely precision

predator
animal that preys on others for food; person who exploits others
predatory

predecessor
former holder of an office or position

predict
to say what will happen in the future
predictability predictable predictably prediction

prefer
to like better; to bring charges before a law-court
preferable preferably preference preferential preferred preferring

pregnant
having a child or young developing in the womb; meaningful
pregnancy pregnancies

prejudice
opinion formed without full information; bias;
(to cause to have a) prejudice
prejudiced prejudicial prejudicing

preliminary
preparatory (item)
preliminaries

premature
happening or done too early

premier
prime minister; first in importance
premiership

première
first performance of a film, play, etc.; to give a première of
premièred premièring

premises
building and land

premium
regular sum paid for insurance policy; bonus
premiums

preparation
preparing; something mixed ready for use

prepare
to make ready; to assemble
preparatory preparing

preposition
word used with a noun or pronoun to show direction, time, etc.
prepositional

prescribe
to set down a rule; to recommend the use of medicine
prescribable prescribing prescriptive

prescription
prescribing, esp. of medicine

presence
being present; dignified bearing

present[1]
existing now; (of the) time that is now
presently

present[2]
gift; to introduce or offer
presentable presentably presentation

preserve
to keep safe; to protect from decay; fruit jam
preservable preservation preservative preserver preserving

president
head of state of a republic;
leader of a meeting, club, etc.
preside presidency presidencies presidential presiding

press
to push steadily against;
to force; newspapers, etc., collectively;
machine for pressing
presses

pressure
pressing force; urgent demands
pressurize or *pressurise*

prestige
good reputation gained from success, wealth, etc.
prestigious

presume
to suppose; to take advantage of
presumable presumably presuming presumption

pretend
to create a false appearance of
pretence (US *pretense*)

pretty
attractive; quite
prettier prettiest prettily prettiness

prevail
to be superior; to occur widely
prevalence prevalent prevailing

prevent
to stop from happening or doing
preventable prevention preventive

previous
coming before
previously

prey
animal hunted as food;
to hunt or kill as prey
preyed preying

price
sum of money for which something is bought or sold;
to put a price on
priceless pricey pricing

prick
to make a small mark or hole in with a sharp point

pride
conceit; (to have a sense of) self-respect; group of lions
priding

priest
member of the Christian clergy; (fem. **priestess**) person who performs religious ceremonies in non-Christian religions
priesthood priestly

primary
most important; first;
preliminary US election
primaries primarily

prime
most important; to prepare for use
primer priming

primitive
of an early stage of development;
unsophisticated

prince
male member of a royal family, esp. the son of a sovereign; ruler of a state
princedom princely principality principalities

princess
female member of a royal family, esp. the daughter of a sovereign; wife of a prince

principal
chief; head of a school or other institution; sum of money on which interest is paid
principally

principle
rule or standard, as of general behaviour; basic truth; general law
principled

print
to reproduce books, etc., by applying ink to paper, etc.; to write in capital letters
printable printer printing printout

prior
previous

priority
(thing taking) precedence
priorities prioritize or *prioritise*

prison
building in which criminals are confined
prisoner

private
of an individual, not public; confidential; soldier of the lowest rank
privacy privately privatize or *privatise*

privilege
special right or advantage
privileged

prize
reward, esp. for winning a contest; to value highly
prizing

probable
likely to happen or be true
probability probabilities probably

problem
something that is difficult to solve, understand, or deal with
problematic problematically

procedure
(established) method
procedural procedurally

proceed
to go on; to continue or advance
proceedings

process
series of actions; method; legal action; to treat or deal with
processes processor

procession
line of people or vehicles moving forward in an orderly manner
processional

produce
to bring into existence; to manufacture; something produced, esp. crops, vegetables, and fruit
producer producing

product
something produced; result of multiplying numbers
production producing; amount produced; work prepared and ready for the stage

productive
producing goods or services; fertile or fruitful
productivity

profession
occupation; open statement of belief

professional
(person who is) paid to do a job; of a high standard
professionalism professionally

professor
highest-ranking academic in a university department
professorial

profile
side view of a person's head; brief outline

profit
gain or benefit, esp. financial; to gain a profit
profited profiteer profiting

profitable
producing a profit; useful or fruitful
profitability profitably

profound
very deep
profundity profundities

program
set of instructions for a computer; to supply a computer with instructions; (US) *programme*
programmer programming

programme (US **program**)
plan or list of items or events; to plan as part of a programme
programmed (US *programed*)
programming (US *programing*)

progress
(to) advance
progresses progression progressive

prohibit
to forbid
prohibition prohibitionism prohibitionist prohibitive

project
to jut out; (to plan a) scheme
projection projectionist projector

prominent
conspicuous; distinguished; jutting-out
prominence prominently

promiscuous
indulging in many casual sexual relationships
promiscuity

promise
(to give a) declaration assuring one will do or not do something; (to show) potential
promising

promote
to raise in position or rank; to further or encourage
promoter promoting promotion promotional

prompt
punctual; to help an actor remember the next words
prompter promptitude promptly

prone
lying face down; inclined (to)

pronoun
word used in place of a noun
pronominal

pronounce
to articulate; to declare officially
pronounceable pronouncement pronouncing pronunciation

proof
evidence that shows something to be true; measure of the strength of alcoholic drink; trial printing impression

propel
to drive or move forwards
propellant propelled propeller propelling

proper
suitable or right
properly

property
something owned, esp. a building; things someone owns; quality or feature
properties

proportion
part; suitable relationship between a part and the whole
proportional proportionally proportionate proportionately

propose
to put forward for consideration; to make an offer of marriage
proposal proposer proposing

proposition
proposal or statement; to suggest sexual intercourse to

prose
ordinary written language or speech, not verse
prosaic prosy

prosecute
to take legal action against
prosecuting prosecution prosecutor

prospect
view; expectation or possibility; to explore in search of
prospective prospector

prosper
to do well, esp. to be come wealthy
prosperity prosperous

protect
to defend; to help home industries
protection protectionism protectionist protective protector

protein
complex organic compound that is an essential constituent of all living cells

protest
(to make a) statement or expression of disapproval
protestation protester

proud
conceited or haughty; having self-respect
proudly

prove
to provide proof of; to test the quality of
provable proven proving

proverb
old short wise saying
proverbial proverbially

provide
to supply
provider providing

provided or **providing**
if; on condition (that)

province
administrative division of a country; area or sphere of activity
provincial

provision
providing

provisional
temporary or conditional
provisionally

provisions
food and drink

provoke
to anger; to stimulate
provocation provocative provoking

prudent
wise or cautious
prudence prudently

psychiatry
study of mental disorders
psychiatric psychiatrist

psychology
study of the mind and mental processes
psychological psychologically psychologist

pub
(informal) public house

public
for the people generally, not private; people in the community

publication
act of publishing; published work

publicity
notices, etc., to gain public attention
publicize or *publicise*

publish
to produce a book, etc., and sell and distribute it to the public
publisher publishes

pudding
dessert, esp. cooked mixture of flour, milk, and eggs

pull
to exert force on something so as to draw it towards the source of the force; power or influence

pullover
knitted garment that is pulled on over the head

pulse
rhythmic throbbing of the arteries by the contractions of the heart; to throb rhythmically
pulsate pulsation pulsing

pump
device for forcing liquid, air, etc., into or out of something; to transfer by using a pump

punch
to strike with the fist; to make a hole in; blow with the fist; tool used to make holes
punches

punctual
arriving or happening at the agreed time
punctuality punctually

punctuation
marks such as a full stop and a comma added to written material
punctuate punctuating

punish
to cause to suffer for a crime
punishable punishes punishment punitive

pupil
schoolchild taught by a teacher; opening in the centre of the iris of the eye

puppet
small doll moved by strings or that fits over the hand
puppeteer puppetry

puppy
young dog
puppies

purchase
to buy; something that is bought
purchaser purchasing

pure
fee from other, esp. contaminating, materials
purely purify purist purity

purple
colour made by mixing red and blue

purpose
reason for doing something or intention; determination; to intend
purposeful purposeless purposely purposing

purse
small bag for money; to pucker the lips
pursing

pursue
to chase in order to catch; to carry on
pursuance pursuant pursued pursuer pursuing pursuit

push
to exert force on something so as to move it away from the source of the force; act of *pushing*
pushes pusher pushing pushy

put
to place in a certain position; to throw
putting

puzzle
game designed to test one's skill; to perplex
puzzler puzzling

pyjamas (US **pajamas**)
loose lightweight jacket and trousers for sleeping in

pyramid
structure with a flat square base and sloping sides that meet at a point
pyramidal

Qq

quack
(to make the) characteristic sound of a duck; unqualified person claiming to be a doctor
quackery

quaint
attractively old-fashioned

qualify
to make eligible for; to modify the meaning of
qualification qualified qualifier qualifies qualifying

quality
characteristic; (degree of) excellence
qualities qualitative

quantity
(large) amount
quantities quantifiable quantify quantitative

quarrel
(to have an) angry disagreement
quarrelled (US *quarreled*) *quarreller* (US *quarreler*) *quarrelling* (US *quarreling*) *quarrelsome*

quarry[1]
large open pit from which minerals are excavated; to extract from a quarry
quarries quarried quarrying

quarry[2]
animal or person that is hunted
quarries

quarter
one of 4 equal parts; coin worth 25 cents; to cut into quarters
quarterly

quay
landing-place for loading and unloading ships

queen
female sovereign ruler; wife of a king

queer
odd; unwell or faint; (informal) homosexual person

query
(to) question; to express doubt about
queries queried querying

question
expression designed to draw out information; matter under discussion; to ask or interrogate
questionable questionably questioner questioning

questionnaire
set of questions used in gathering statistics

queue
line of people, etc., waiting; to wait in a queue
queued queuing

quick
performed or happening in a short time; fast-moving
quicken quickie quickly

quid
(informal) pound sterling

quiet
marked by the absence of noise; peaceful
quieten quietly quietude

quit
to give up; to go away from
quitted or *quit quitter quitting*

quite
completely; fairly

quiz
series of questions to test knowledge
quizzes quizzed quizzing

quota
fixed share or proportion; upper limit
quotas

quote
to repeat a phrase or passage; to estimate costs; passage quoted; estimate of costs
quotable quotation quoting

Rr

a b c d e f g h i j k l m n o p q **r** s t u v w x y z

rabbit
(to hunt a) long-eared burrowing animal; (*informal*) to talk boringly
rabbited rabbiting

race[1]
(to compete in a) contest
racer racing

race[2]
group of people with common characteristics; major division of humankind
racial racialism racialist racially racism racist

rack
framework for storing and displaying objects; to cause to suffer

racket[1] or **racquet**
bat with interlaced strings used in tennis, etc.

racket[2]
great noise; commotion; illegal enterprise
racketeer racketeering

radar
system for detecting the position of an object by means of high-frequency radio waves

radiate
to send out light, heat, etc.; to display
radiating radiation

radiator
appliance that radiates heat; cooling appliance in an internal-combustion engine

radical
fundamental; wanting drastic political, etc., changes
radicalism radically

radio
broadcasting system for sound; apparatus for receiving broadcast signals; to send a signal by radio
radios radioed radioing

rag
piece of old cloth
ragged raggedly

rage
(to express) violent anger; craze
raging

raid
(to make a) sudden attack

rail
horizontal bar of wood, etc.; either of the 2 lengths of steel that form a railway

railway
track consisting of 2 rails on which trains run

rain
drops of water that fall from the clouds

rainbow
coloured arc that appears in the sky when the sun shines through rain

raise
to lift up; to rear
raising

raisin
dried grape

rally
mass meeting; to come together
rallies rallied rallying

ram
uncastrated male sheep; battering beam; to collide with deliberately
rammed ramming

ramble
to stroll about; leisurely walk
rambler rambling

ran
past tense of **run**

ranch
large North American cattle farm
ranches

random
without plan or order
randomly

rang
past tense of **ring**

range
extent or scope; selection of products; to place in a row; to vary between limits
ranger ranging

rank
position in a scale; status; to assign to a rank

rap
(to strike with a) sharp light blow
rapped rapping

rape
forcing a person to have sexual intercourse against his or her will; to commit rape on
raping rapist

rapid
quick
rapidity rapidly

rare
uncommon; lightly cooked
rarely rarity rarities

raspberry
kind of (shrub bearing) edible purplish-red fruit
raspberries

rat
mouse-like rodent; to betray one's friend, etc.
ratted ratting ratty

rate
charge or amount in relation to a unit; local authority tax; to consider the value of
rateable or *ratable rating*

rather
slightly; preferably

ratio
relation between 2 numbers or amounts
ratios

ration
(to limit to a) fixed amount

rational
using reason; sensible
rationalism rationality rationalize or *rationalise rationally*

rattle
(to make a) series of short sharp sounds; toy that rattles
rattling rattly

raw
uncooked; not processed; inexperienced

ray
thin beam of light; trace

razor
shaving instrument

reach
to arrive at; to extend; distance
reaches reachable

react
to act in response to something
reaction reactive reactor

read
to be able to understand written words
readability readable reader readership reading

ready
prepared for use or action
readier readiest readily readiness

real
existing; true; natural
really

realism
awareness and acceptance of things as they are; artistic and literary style
realist realistic realistically

reality
actually existing state of affairs; fact
realities

realize or **realise**
to understand or grasp; to turn into a fact; to convert into money
realizable or *realisable realization* or *realisation realizing* or *realising*

realm
kingdom; sphere or field

rear[1]
back (part)

rear[2]
to care for; (of a horse) to rise on its hind legs

reason
cause or explanation;
to think or persuade logically

reasonable
sensible; fair
reasonably

reassure
to restore confidence to
reassurance reassuring

rebel
to oppose authority;
person who rebels
rebelled rebelling rebellion rebellious rebelliously

recall
to remember; to call back; memory

recede
to withdraw; to slope backwards
receding

receipt
written acknowledgement of receiving payment

receive
to accept; to welcome visitors
receivable receiver receiving

recent
happening not long ago; modern or new
recently

reception
receiving; formal party or welcome
receptionist

recession
decline in economic activity

recipe
set of cooking instructions

reckon
to calculate; to think
reckoning

recognize or **recognise**
to identify; to realize or acknowledge
recognition recognizable or *recognisable recognizably* or *recognisably recognizing* or *recognising*

recommend
to advise; to speak favourably about
recommendable recommendation

reconcile
to put on friendly terms again; to cause to accept
reconcilable reconciliation reconciling

reconnaissance
preliminary survey of an area
reconnoitre (US *reconnoiter*) *reconnoitring* (US *reconnoitering*)

reconstruct
to build again; to re-create an event
reconstruction

record
flat disc on which sound is recorded; written account; best performance; to copy sound; to set down in writing
recorded recorder recording

recount[1]
to tell or narrate

re-count or **recount**[2]
to count again; second count

recover[1]
to return to a healthy condition
recoverable recovery

re-cover or **recover**[2]
to cover again

re-create or **recreate**
to create again

recreation
relaxation; leisure activity
recreational

recruit
(to enlist a) new soldier, member, or supporter
recruitment

recycle
to process into a useful product
recyclable recycling

red
of the colour of blood
redden redder reddest reddish red-hot

reduce
to lessen; to bring into a particular condition
reducible reducing reduction

redundant
unnecessary; no longer needed
redundancy redundancies

reed
tall grass-like plant;
vibrating part in wind instrument
reedy

reel
cylindrical device on to which tape, etc., is wound; winding device on a fishing rod; to wind on a reel; to whirl about or sway

refer
to speak about; to consult;
to direct (to)
referable reference referral referred referring

referee
official who supervises the playing of a game such as football; person bearing witness to someone's character; to act as a referee
refereed refereeing

referendum
direct vote on a political issue by an electorate
referendums or *referenda*

reflect
to throw back light, etc.;
to ponder
reflection or *reflexion reflective reflector*

reflexive
(grammar) (of a word) referring to the agent or subject

reform
to change for the better; improvement
reformation reformatory reformatories reformer

refrain[1]
to stop oneself from doing

refrain[2]
regularly repeated lines of a song

refresh
to restore the vitality of
refreshes refreshing refreshment

refrigerator
domestic appliance that keeps food cool
refrigerate refrigerating refrigeration

refugee
person who flees for safety to a foreign country

refuse[1]
to say one is unwilling
refusal refusing

refuse[2]
waste or rubbish

regard
to look closely at;
to consider; respect

regarding
concerning

regardless
despite everything; unconcerned

regime
system of government

region
(administrative) area or district
regional regionally

register
list or record; to enter in a register
registration registry registries

regret
to be very sorry for; feeling of sorrow and remorse
regretful regrettable regrettably regretted regretting

regular
usual or normal; occurring at fixed points of time
regularity regularize or *regularise regularly*

regulate
to adjust; to control by rules
regulating regulator

regulation
regulating; rule

rehearse
to practise a play, piece of music, etc., before the performance
rehearsal rehearsing

reign
monarch's period of rule; to rule as a monarch

rein
long strap attached to a horse's bridle; to control with a rein

reinforce
to make stronger
reinforcement reinforcing

reject
to refuse to accept; to discard
rejection

relate
to tell or narrate; to connect
related relating

relation
connection; relative

relationship
(personal) connection

relative
measured in relation to something else; person related to another; (grammar) referring to a preceding noun or clause
relatively relativity

relax
to make or become less tense
relaxant relaxation relaxes

release
to set free; to make widely known or available; something made widely known or available
releasing

relevant
connected with the matter in hand
relevance or *relevancy relevantly*

reliable
dependable
reliability reliably reliance

relief
lessening of pain or worry; worker who takes over from another; carving in which the design stands out from its background

relieve
to lessen pain or worry; to take over from another person
relieving

religion
belief in and worship of God
religiosity religious religiously

reluctant
unwilling; disinclined
reluctance reluctantly

rely
to depend (on); to trust
reliable reliance relied relies *relying*

remain
to continue to be; to be left
remainder remains

remark
(to) comment or notice

remarkable
noteworthy
remarkably

remedy
cure; to put right
remedies remedial remedied remedying

remember
to keep in the memory; to bring to mind
remembrance

remind
to cause to remember
reminder

reminisce
to talk about old times
reminiscence reminiscent reminiscing

remorse
feeling of sorrow for things done wrong in the past
remorseful remorsefully remorseless remorselessly

remote
distant
remotely remoteness remoter remotest

remove
to take away or off; to move to a new location
removable removal removing

rendezvous
arranged meeting; to meet at a specified time or place
rendezvoused rendezvousing

renew
to make new; to extend
renewable renewal

rent
regular payment for the use of something
rentable rental

repair
to mend; state or condition
repairable

repeat
to do or say again
repeatable
repetition repetitious repetitive
repetitively

repertoire
dramas, etc., that a company or actor is prepared to perform

replace
to put back in its place; to take the place of
replaceable replacement replacing

reply
(to) answer
replies replied replying

report
(to give an) account, statement, or description
reporter

represent
to act on behalf of; to describe; to stand for
representation representative

reproduce
to produce a copy of; to produce young or offspring
reproducing reproduction
reproductive

reptile
cold-blooded air-breathing vertebrate animal
reptilian

republic
form of government in which the people or their elected representatives possess the supreme power
republican republicanism

reputation
overall opinion of a person, organization, etc.
reputable repute reputedly reputing

request
to ask for; thing asked for

require
to need or demand
requirement requiring

rescue
to free from danger; instance of rescuing
rescuable rescuer rescuing

research
(to undertake) careful study
researches researcher

resemble
to be like
resemblance resembling

reservation
reserving; booking; qualification

reserve
to set aside for later or special use; auxiliary military force; land set aside for animals
reserved reserving

residence
place in which one lives; home
reside residency residencies *resident*
residential residing

resign
to give up
resignation resigned resignedly

resist
to withstand; to fight against
resistance resistant resister resistible

resolute
determined; steadfast
resolution

resolve
to decide firmly; to solve a problem; to separate into parts; determination
resolving

resort
to turn (to); holiday centre

resource
means of help or support; supply

respect
(to hold in) high regard; aspect or detail
respectful respectfully

respectable
decent, worthy, or acceptable
respectability respectably

respective
relating to each separately
respectively

respond
to answer; to react
respondent

response
responding; reply
responsive

responsible
answerable (to); important; trustworthy
responsibility responsibilities responsibly

rest[1]
to stop work, etc.; to lie down; relaxation; support
restful

rest[2]
to remain; remainder

restaurant
commercial establishment where meals are bought and eaten
restaurateur

restless
agitated; fidgety
restlessly restlessness

restore
to return (to its original condition); to bring back
restorable restoration restorative restorer restoring

restrain
to hold back forcibly
restraint

restrict
to confine or regulate
restriction restrictive

result
(to occur as an) outcome; answer to a calculation
resultant

resume
to start again
resuming resumption

resuscitate
to revive
resuscitating resuscitation

retail
(of or associated with the) sale of goods to the general public
retailer

retain
to continue to keep
retention retentive

retire
to give up one's work;
to withdraw to a quieter place; to go to bed
retirement retiring

retreat
to withdraw; (period of) rest and meditation

retrieve
to get back again;
to bring back
retrievable retrieval retriever retrieving

return
to go or come back; to take back;
profit or proceeds
returnable returner

reveal
to make known; to uncover
revealing revelation

revenge
retaliatory act; vengeance;
to avenge
revengeful revenging

revenue
income, esp. government income from taxes

reverse
to put the opposite way round; to move backwards; opposite
reversal reversible reversing

review
to examine again; (to undertake a) survey or critical report of a book, etc.
reviewer

revise
to consider and amend;
to study for an examination
revising revision

revive
to return to life, consciousness, activity, etc.
revival reviving

revolt
to rebel; to disgust
revolting

revolution
overthrow of a government, etc.;
single rotation
revolutionary revolutionaries
revolutionize or revolutionise

revolve
to turn on an axis
revolver revolving

reward
(to give) something offered in return for a service or good deed
rewarding

rhubarb
kind of garden plant with long edible stalks

rhyme
(to form a) correspondence in the sound of words
rhyming

rhythm
pattern of recurring beats or emphases in music or speech
rhythmic rhythmical rhythmically

ribbon
narrow strip of fine fabric, etc.

rice
kind of grass whose grains are used as food

rich
wealthy

riches
wealth

rid
(to) free (of)
riddance ridded or *rid ridding*

ride
to sit on a horse, bicycle, etc., and control its movements; to be carried by a bus, etc.
ridden rider riding rode

ridge
raised strip, esp. of land

ridiculous
absurd
ridicule ridiculing ridiculously

rifle
firearm with long grooved barrel

right
correct or proper; opposite of left; having conservative political views; to return to an upright position; just entitlement
rightful rightfully rightist rightwards

rigid
strict; stiff
rigidity rigidly

rigorous
strict or harsh
rigour (US *rigor*)

rim
(to form or cover the) outer edge of a circular opening
rimmed rimming

ring[1]
circular band of metal worn on a finger; circle; enclosed area where circus acts are performed; to surround
ringed ringing

ring[2]
to (cause to) sound like a bell; (informal) to telephone; telephone call
rang ringing rung

riot
(to take part in a) wild disturbance
rioted rioter rioting riotous

rip
(to) tear; to rush on
ripped ripping

ripe
mature; ready to be eaten or used
ripen riper ripest

rise
to increase; to go upwards; to get up; increase; upward slope
risen riser rising rose

risk
(to expose to the) possibility of loss, injury, or damage
riskier riskiest riskily riskiness risky

rival
person or group that competes with another; to be as good as
rivalled (US *rivaled*) *rivalling* (US *rivaling*) *rivalry rivalries*

river
large natural stream of flowing water

road
open surfaced way for vehicles

roar
(to utter a) long deep cry

roast
to cook by dry heat in an oven

rob
to steal from
robbed robber robbery robberies robbing

robot
machine that performs tasks automatically, esp. in the manner of human beings
robotic

rock[1]
solid part of the earth's crust; large mass of stone
rockery rockeries rocky

rock[2]
to move form side to side

rocket
self-propelling device, esp. used to launch a spacecraft; to increase or move very fast
rocketed rocketing rocketry

rod
straight thin pole

rode
past tense of **ride**

role
actor's part; function

roll
to move by turning over and over; small rounded cake of bread

romance
love affair; captivating atmosphere; to compose or tell strongly imaginative stories
romancer romancing romantic romantically romanticism romanticize or *romanticise*

roof
(to put on the) cover of a building
roofs or *rooves roofing*

room
enclosed area in a building; space
roomier roomiest roomy

root
part of a plant that holds it in the ground and absorbs food; source; to send down roots into the ground

rope
(to fasten with a) strong thick cord
roping ropy

rose[1]
past tense of **rise**

rose[2]
kind of garden shrub with a thorny stem and showy flowers

rot
(to) decay
rotted rotter rotting

rotate
to turn on an axis
rotatable rotating rotation

rotten
decayed; (informal) unpleasant

rough
not even; not gentle; violent; coarse
roughage roughen roughly

round
(to make) circular; (one in a) set; stage in a tournament; on all sides of

roundabout
merry-go-round; road junction at which traffic moves in a circle

route
(to send by a) course taken to get to a destination
routeing

routine
usual procedure

row[1]
arrangement in line

row[2]
to propel a boat with oars
rowed rowing

row[3]
(to) quarrel; loud noise

royal
of, belonging to, or suitable for a king or queen
royalist royally royalty

rub
to move something backwards and forwards over a surface
rubbed rubbing

rubber
elastic substance from certain plants; pencil eraser
rubbery

rubbish
worthless matter
rubbishy

rude
not polite; primitive
rudely rudeness ruder rudest

rug
floor covering

rugby
form of football played with an oval ball

ruin
state of collapse; destroyed building; to bring to ruin
ruination ruinous ruinously

rule
principle; authority; to govern or control; to draw a straight line
ruler ruling

rumour (US **rumor**)
information, which may not be true, that is passed on verbally

run
to move quickly; to flow; enclosure for animals; point in cricket, etc.
ran
runner running runny

rung[1]
past participle of **ring**[2]

rung[2]
crosspiece of a ladder

rural
of the country

rush[1]
to move forward quickly; sudden forceful movement
rushes

rush[2]
tall grass-like plant growing near water
rushes

rust
reddish-brown coating forming on iron, etc., when exposed to air and moisture; to affect with rust; to deteriorate through lack of use
rustier rustiest rusty

Ss

sack
large bag made of coarse cloth, etc.; to plunder; (informal) to dismiss from employment

sacred
dedicated to a god; holy

sacrifice
(to make an) offering to a god; to give up for the sake of something else
sacrificial sacrificing

sacrilege
violation of something sacred
sacrilegious

sad
unhappy; regrettable
sadder saddest sadly sadness

saddle
leather seat on the back of a horse; bicycle seat; to put a saddle on; to burden
saddler saddlery

safe
giving protection; not in danger; container for safe storage of valuables
safely safer safest safety

said
past tense and past participle of **say**

sail
sheet of strong material to catch the wind on a boat; to travel on the water

sailor
member of a ship's crew

saint
holy person
sainthood saintliness saintly

sake
benefit or purpose

salad
cold dish of lettuce, tomatoes, etc.

salary
(esp. monthly) payment for regular work
salaries salaried

sale
act of selling; selling of goods at reduced prices
saleable or *salable salesman salesmanship salesperson saleswoman*

salt
white powder or solid used as a flavouring or preservative; chemical compound formed by the action of an acid on metal; to season with salt
saltier saltiest saltiness salty

same
identical; being previously mentioned

sample
(to take a) small representative part
sampler sampling

sanction
(to give an) authorization; coercive measure taken against a country, etc.

sand
fine particles of rock; beach; to smooth with sandpaper
sandy

sandwich
2 or more slices of bread with a filling; to insert between 2 things
sandwiches

sane
not made; reasonable
saner sanest sanity

sang
past tense of **sing**

sank
past tense of **sink**

sash
brightly coloured band of cloth; frame containing panes in a window
sashes

sat
past tense and past participle of **sit**

satchel
bag with shoulder strap for carrying school books

satellite
celestial body orbiting a planet; man-made device orbiting a celestial body

satire
piece of writing in which people or things are ridiculed
satirical satirically satirist satirize or *satirise*

satisfaction
state of being satisfied

satisfactory
satisfying needs; acceptable
satisfactorily

satisfy
to make contented; to provide enough for; to convince
satisfied satisfies satisfying

Saturday
7th day of the week

sauce
liquid preparation served with some foods; impudence
saucier sauciest saucepan saucy

saucer
small round dish on which a cup is set

sausage
minced meat, etc., stuffed into a tube-shaped casing

savage
wild; fierce; to attack wildly
savagely savagery savaging

save
to rescue; to put aside for future use
saver saving

savings
money put aside for future use

savoury (US **savory**)
(of) food having a salty or spicy taste
savouries (US *savories*)

saw[1]
past tense of **see**

saw[2]
(to cut with a) tool with a sharp-toothed blade
sawed sawing sawn

say
to speak or utter

said
saying says

saying
proverb or familiar phrase

scale[1]
thin hard plate covering a fish or reptile; coating of lime or dirt; to remove scale(s) from
scaling scaly

scale[2]
one of the pans of a balance

scale[3]
graduated series of marks for measuring; set of musical notes; to climb
scaling

scan
to read through quickly; to examine closely
scanned scanner scanning

scandal
malicious gossip; (discredit produced by) outrageous behaviour
scandalize or *scandalise scandalous scandalously*

scar
mark left after an injury has healed; to make a mark like a scar on
scarred scarring

scarce
rare; not abundant
scarcely scarcity

scare
to fill with fear; sudden attack of fear
scaring scary

scarf
piece of cloth worn round the neck for warmth or decoration
scarves

scarlet
bright red

scatter
to throw about or send in all directions

scene
place where something happens; view or landscape; division of an act in a play
scenic scenically

scenery
attractive natural landscape; backdrops on a theatre stage

scent
pleasant smell; perfume; to detect by smelling

sceptic (US **skeptic**)
person who doubts
sceptical (US *skeptical*) *sceptically* (US *skeptically*) *scepticism* (US *skepticism*)

schedule
(to draw up a) plan, esp. showing the times at which things happen
scheduling

scheme
plan or arrangement; (to) plot
schemer scheming

schizophrenia
mental disorder, esp. causing personality confusion
schizoid schizophrenic

scholar
schoolchild; learned person
scholarly scholarship scholastic scholastically

school
institution where children are taught; group of fish; to teach or discipline
schooling

science
systematic study, esp. dealing with the material and physical universe
scientific scientifically scientist

scissors
cutting implement with 2 crossing blades

scold
to reprimand fiercely

scoop
(to take up with a) long-handled implement with a round bowl; news reported in a newspaper before its competitors

scooter
light motorcycle; child's toy vehicle

scope
opportunity for action; range of influence, etc.

scorch
to burn so as to discolour
scorches

score
record of points made by different players or teams in a game; to gain points in a game; to cut a line into; set of 20; written copy of a musical composition
scorer scoring

scorn
(to show) open contempt
scornful scornfully

scout
person sent to gain information; member of worldwide movement for boys

scramble
to move or climb quickly; to cook eggs by stirring in the pan; to make a message unintelligible
scrambler scrambling

scrap
fragment; waste material; (to) fight or quarrel; to throw away
scrapped scrappier scrappiest scrapping scrappy

scrape
to move a rough object across a surface, esp. to clean or smooth it
scraper scraping

scratch
to mark a surface with a sharp instrument; mark made by scratching; to scrape with the fingernails to relieve itching
scratches

scream
(to utter a) long piercing cry of pain, fear, etc.

screen
light movable frame; surface on to which images, etc., are projected; to shelter

screw
(to fasten things together using a) tapering threaded metal rod; to twist

scribble
to write quickly and carelessly
scribbler scribbling

script
handwriting; written text

scrub[1]
to rub with a stiff brush in order to clean
scrubbed scrubbing

scrub[2]
(land covered with) bushes and stunted trees, etc.
scrubby

scrupulous
very precise; principled
scruple

scrutiny
close and detailed examination
scrutineer scrutinize or *scrutinise*

sculpture
art of carving stone, etc., into shapes; to carve in this way
sculpt sculptor sculptural sculpturing

sea
large body of salt water

seal[1]
kind of sea mammal with flippers

seal[2]
piece of wax used to keep a parcel closed; tight, esp. airtight, closure; to close tightly
sealant

seam
line formed where 2 pieces of material are sewn together; layer of coal, etc.
seamless

search
to look for; to examine thoroughly; act of searching
searches searcher

seaside
area beside the sea, esp. as visited by holidaymakers

season
one of the 4 periods of the year; to flavour food
seasonal seasonally seasoning

seat
chair, stool, etc.; to cause to sit; location for something

second[1]
next after first
secondly

second[2]
60th part of a minute

second[3]
to support
seconder

second[4]
to release an official, etc., temporarily to another department

secondary
of lesser importance
secondarily

second-hand
previously owned by someone else; from a previous owner; indirectly through someone else

secret
(something) kept hidden from the knowledge of other people
secrecy secretive secretively secretiveness secretly

secretary
person who deals with correspondence, filing, etc., in an office; head of a government department
secretaries secretarial secretariat secretaryship

secrete[1]
(of a gland) to produce and release fluid
secreting secretion

secrete[2]
to put in a hidden place
secreting secretion

section
part or division; representative sample
sectional

sector
division or part; part of a circle between 2 radii

secure
(to make) safe; to obtain
securely securing security *securities*

see
to (be able to) perceive with the eyes
saw seeing seen

seed
part of a plant, etc., that is capable of germination to produce a new plant, etc.

seek
to try to find
sought

seem
to appear (to be)
seemingly

seen
past participle of **see**

segment
part or piece that has been separated or cut off
segmental segmentary segmentation

segregate
to separate different groups
segregating segregation

seize
to take hold of forcefully; to become jammed
seizing seizure

seldom
rarely

select
to choose; chosen; very good
selection selective selectively

self
individual's own character, etc.
selves selfless

selfish
caring only about one's own interests
selfishly selfishness

sell
to transfer in exchange for money
seller sold

senate
upper assembly in legislative body of some countries; governing body of some universities
senator senatorial

send
to cause to be taken or conveyed
sender sent

senior
older; higher in rank
seniority

sensation
perception through the senses; (something causing) excitement
sensational sensationalism sensationalist sensationally

sense
power of sight, touch, etc.; to notice; meaning
senseless sensing sensor

sensibility
capacity to feel or perceive
sensibilities

sensible
marked by good judgement or reason
sensibly

sensitive
capable of sensing; easily offended; delicate
sensitively sensitivity sensitize or *sensitise*

sent
past tense and past participle of **send**

sentence
self-contained group of words; (to impose a) judgement in a court
sentencing

sentiment
thought; (excessive) emotion
sentimental sentimentality
sentimentalize or *sentimentalise*
sentimentally

separate
to move apart; not connected; divided
separable separating separation separatist separator

September
9th month of the year

sequel
something that follows; consequence
sequence

sergeant
rank in the army or police force

serial
(story) presented or performed in several parts; of a series
serialize or *serialise serially*

series
group of related things in succession

serious
solemn; sincere; crucial
seriously seriousness

servant
employee who performs household duties

serve
to work for; to attend to customers; to function (as); to be a member of the armed forces
server serving

service
help; (to undertake an) overhaul of a vehicle or appliance; one of the armed forces
serviceable servicing

session
meeting, esp. of a law-court, parliament, etc.

set
to put or present; to apply; to adjust; group of similar things; television or radio receiver; stage scenery
setting

setting
background; place where an event or story takes place; arrangement of cutlery, etc., on a table

settle
to put in a fixed position; to make or become calm; to pay a bill, etc.
settlement settler settling

seven
number 7
seventh

seventeen
number 17
seventeenth

seventy
number 70
seventies seventieth

several
some; different
severally

severe
harsh; extreme
severely severer severest severity severities

sew
to join by means of stitches made with a needle and thread
sewed sewer sewing sewn

sex
male or female; physical desires or activity resulting from sex
sexes sexist sexual sexuality sexy

shabby
dirty; broken-down; mean
shabbier shabbiest shabbily shabbiness

shade
partial darkness produced by the blocking out of light; to protect from the heat or light of the sun; (darker) colour
shading

shadow
dark image caused by something cutting off rays of light; to watch and follow someone closely
shadowy

shady
giving shade; dark; disreputable
shadier shadiest shadily shadiness

shaft
long handle of a spear, etc.; rotating rod that transmits power or motion; long narrow, esp. vertical passage

shake
to move up and down or from side to side quickly
shakeable or *shakable shaken shaker shaky shook*

shall
auxiliary verb used to form the future tense and to express determination
should

shallow
not deep
shallower shallowest

shame
feeling caused by awareness of guilt, failure, etc.; to cause to feel shame
shamefaced shameful shameless shaming

shampoo
(to clean or wash one's hair with a) preparation of soap
shampoos shampooed shampooing

shan't
(informal) shall not

shape
outward form or figure; to make or form
shapeless shapely shaping

share
to divide; part or portion; part of the capital or stock of a business company
shareholder sharing

shark
kind of ferocious predatory fish; person who extorts money from others

sharp
having a fine cutting edge or point; perceptive; acute; (of a musical note) higher by a semitone
sharpen sharpener

shatter
to break into many pieces

shave
to remove hair, esp. from the face, with a razor
shaven shaver shaving

she
subject pronoun referring to a female person or animal

shear
to cut or clip hair or fleece from sheep, etc.
sheared or *shorn*

shed[1]
small building; workshop

shed[2]
to allow to flow or fall
shedding

she'd
(informal) she would; she had

sheep
kind of grass-eating animal that has a thick woolly fleece

sheer
perpendicular; very steep; utter

sheet
large flat thin piece, esp. of cotton, etc., for use as a bed-cover

shelf
narrow board attached horizontally to a wall
shelves

shell
(to remove the) protective hard casing of an egg or nut; (to attack with a) metal case containing explosives

she'll
(informal) she will

shelter
(to provide) protection or safety; structure that keeps off rain, etc.

shelve
to put on a shelf; to postpone; to slope gradually
shelving

shepherd
(fem. **shepherdess**)
person who looks after sheep

sheriff
(US) chief law-enforcing officer in a county; (Brit) chief executive officer of the Crown in a county

she's
(informal) she is; she has

shield
strong piece of body armour carried on the arm; to protect

shift
to move position; to remove with difficulty; group of workers working during a particular period

shine
to emit a steady light; to be outstanding; to polish
shined or *shone shining shiny*

ship
(to transport by a) large sea-going vessel
shipped shipper shipping

shirt
garment worn on the upper part of the body

shiver
to tremble; to break into tiny pieces
shivery

shock
(to cause someone to experience a) sudden disturbance of the mind or feelings; impact
shockable shocker shocking

shoe
(to provide with) one of a pair of coverings for the feet; to fix horseshoes on a horse
shod shoeing

shone
past tense and past participle of **shine**

shook
past tense of **shake**

shoot
to hit or wound with a bullet, etc.; to move very quickly; to aim at a goal; new growth on a plant
shooting shot

shop
building where goods are sold to the public; to go to a shop to buy goods
shopped shopper shopping

shore
land adjoining the sea, lake, etc.

shorn
past participle of shear

short
not long; insufficient; curt; (of pastry) crumbly
shortage shorten shorter shortest shortly

shorts
short trousers; (US) underpants

shot
past tense and past participle of **shoot**; firing a gun; photograph; attempt to hit, kick, etc., a ball into a goal; hypodermic injection

should
past tense of **shall**, used to express obligation, etc.
shouldn't

shoulder
part of the body where the arm joins the trunk; to bear the burden of

shout
(to give a) loud cry

shove
(to give a) violent push
shoving

show
to make or be clear or visible; to exhibit or display; public exhibition or entertainment
showed showing shown showy

shower
brief fall of rain; device that sprays water on to a person's body; to present in abundance
showery

shrewd
clever; wise

shrink
to make or become smaller, esp. from wetness; to recoil (from)
shrank or *shrunk shrinkage shrinking shrunk or shrunken*

shrug
to raise and drop the shoulders to express ignorance, doubt, etc.
shrugged shrugging

shudder
(to) tremble from horror, fear, etc.

shut
to cover an opening; to close
shutter shutting

shy
withdrawn and timid; to draw back
shied shies shyer shyest shying shyly shyness

sick
likely to vomit; ill
sicken sickly sickness

side
surface or part, esp. at right angles to the front or back; aspect; to support
sideways siding

siege
act of surrounding a city, etc., to force it to surrender

sigh
(to give a) long audible breath

sight
power of seeing; something seen; device that helps to aim
sightless sightseeing sightseer

sign
symbol or gesture; notice; to write one's signature on

signal
sign; device that gives warning; to communicate by signals; notable
signalled (US *signaled*) *signaller* (US *signaler*) *signalling* (US *signaling*) *signally*

signature
person's name, handwritten by that person
signatory signatories

significant
important; having meaning
significance significantly

signify
to mean; to matter
signification signified signifies signifying

silence
(to cause an) absence of noise or sound
silencer silencing

silent
marked by an absence of noise or sound

silhouette
black outline, esp. of a person in profile; to cause to appear in silhouette
silhouetted silhouetting

silk
fine soft fibre produced by silkworms
silken silky

silly
absurd or foolish
sillier silliest silliness

silver
(to coat or plate with a) shining greyish-white metal; articles made of silver; greyish-white colour

similar
resembling or like
similarity similarities similarly

simple
easy; plain; humble
simpler simplest simplicity simply

simplify
to make easier
simplification simplified simplifies simplifying

simultaneous
taking place or functioning at the same time
simultaneity or *simultaneousness simultaneously*

sin
(to commit an) offence against God's law
sinful sinned sinner sinning

since
from a former time until now; as

sincere
genuine; honest
sincerely sincerity

sing
to utter musical sounds
sang singer sung

single
only 1; unmarried; (ticket) for outward journey only; to pick (out)
singling singly

singular
unusual or extraordinary; (grammar) referring to 1 person or thing
singularity singularly

sink
(to cause) to go down below the surface of water; to appear to go down below the horizon; fixed basin in a kitchen
sank sinkable sunk sunken

sip
to drink by taking small mouthfuls; small mouthful
sipped sipping

sir
polite term of address to a man

sister
daughter of the same parents; senior nurse; nun
sisterhood sister-in-law sisters-in-law sisterly

sit
to rest on a seat; to take an examination; to be in session
sat sitter sitting

site
(to provide with an) area of ground for a particular use
siting

situation
position or location; job; circumstances
situate situated

six
number 6
sixth

sixteen
number 16
sixteenth

sixty
number 60
sixties sixtieth

size
set of measurements; to order according to size
sizeable or *sizable sizing*

skate
(boot fitted with a) metal blade for gliding over ice
skater skating

skeleton
hard bony framework of an animal body; bare basic framework
skeletal

sketch
rough quickly drawn plan, etc.; short comic play; to make a sketch of
sketches sketchy

ski
one of a pair of long narrow strips of wood, etc., for gliding over snow
skis skied skier skies skiing

skilful (US **skillful**)
possessing or showing skill
skilfully (US *skillfully*)

skill
ability to do something well
skilled

skin
(to remove the) outer covering of a body, fruit, etc.
skinned skinnier skinniest skinning skinny

skip
to move with quick short jumps; to miss out; container for rubbish
skipped skipping

skirt
girl's or woman's legless garment hanging from the waist; to go along the border of

skull
bony skeleton of the head

sky
upper atmosphere; to hit a ball high into the air
skies skied

slack
not tight or tense; not busy; to be lazy
slacken slacker slackly slackness

slam
to close a door, etc., noisily
slammed slamming

slang
highly informal language; language of a particular group; to abuse verbally
slangy

slap
(to strike with a) sharp blow of the open hand
slapped slapping

slaughter
killing of animals for food; to kill animals for food; to kill cruelly
slaughterer slaughterhouse

slave
person who is owned by and forced to work for another; (informal) to work very hard
slavery slaving slavish

sleep
(to be in a state of) natural suspension of consciousness
sleeping sleepy slept

sleeve
part of a garment covering the arm; cover for a gramophone record
sleeved sleeveless

slender
slim or thin

slice
thin flat piece cut from something; to cut into slices
slicer slicing

slide
to move smoothly; chute; photographic transparency
slid slider sliding

slight
small; not significant; (to) insult
slightly slightness

slim
gracefully thin; small; to make oneself thin by dieting
slimly slimmed slimmer slimmest slimming slimness

slip[1]
to lose one's balance and slide over; to move smoothly; mistake; petticoat
slipped slipping slippy

slip[2]
small piece of paper; plant cutting; young thin person

slipper
light shoe worn in the house

slippery
tending to cause slipping
slipperiness

slit
(to make a) long narrow cut
slitting

slope
(to) slant; hill
sloping

slot
(to insert into a) narrow groove or opening
slotted slotting

slow
not quick; dull or sluggish; showing an earlier time
slower slowest slowly slowness

smack
(to) hit with the open hand; to open the lips noisily

small
not large or great; not important; humble; narrow part of the back
smaller smallest smallness

smart
neat; fashionable; to cause a stinging pain; clever
smarten smartly smartness

smash
to break into pieces; to hit or strike hard; to defeat; act of smashing
smashes smashing

smell
power of perceiving through the nose; to perceive in this way; (to emit an) odour
smelled or *smelt smellier smelliest smelly*

smile
(to show an) amused or happy facial expression
smiling

smoke
visible gas produced from burning; to breathe in and out the fumes of burning tobacco
smoker smokier smokiest smoking smoky

smooth
(to make) even; not rough

snack
quick light meal

snake
(to move like a) long-bodied legless reptile
snaking snaky

snap
to make a cracking noise; to break; to speak angrily; (to take a) photograph; sudden spell of cold weather
snapped snapping snappy

snatch
to seize suddenly; brief part of a conversation, etc.
snatches snatcher

sneeze
(to make a) sudden involuntary expulsion of air from the nose and mouth
sneezing

sniff
to draw air audibly up the nose

snow
ice crystals falling from the sky in white flakes
snowy

so
to such an extent; extremely; in order (that); with the result (that); therefore

soak
to make or become full of a liquid

soap
substance used to remove dirt
soapy

soar
to rise or fly upwards

sober
not drunk; serious; subdued
soberly sobriety

soccer
Association football

social
(preferring) being in groups; of society
socialism socialist socialistic socialite
socialize or *socialise*

society
association or club; people living in an organized community
societies

sock
cloth covering for the foot

socket
device into which an electric plug is fitted to complete a circuit

sofa
long seat with a back and arms

soft
not hard; not loud or glaring; easily moulded; (of drink) non-alcoholic
soften softer softest softly softness

software
programs, etc., that enable computers to work

soil
earth or ground; land; to make dirty

sold
past tense and past participle of **sell**

soldier
(to serve as a) member of an army

sole[1]
underpart of the foot or shoe; to fit with a (new) sole
soling

sole[2]
being the only one
solely

solemn
serious; very formal
solemness solemnity solemnities solemnize or *solemnise solemnly*

solicitor
kind of lawyer; legal officer of a city or state

solid
not hollow; (substance that is) neither liquid nor gas; firm
solidarity solidify solidity solidly

solo
composition for 1 performer
solos soloist

solution
answer to a problem; mixture of a solid and a liquid
soluble

solve
to find an answer to a problem
solvable solving

solvent
able to pay one's debts; (liquid) able to dissolve another substance
solvency

some
any; several; certain; unspecified

somebody
unspecified person

somehow
by some means or other

someone
unspecified person

something
unspecified thing

sometimes
occasionally; not always

somewhat
rather

somewhere
in some unspecified place

son
male child of parents
son-in-law sons-in-law

song
musical composition with words to be sung

soon
in a short time
sooner soonest

sophisticated
refined; high-class; elaborate or complex
sophistication

sore
painful or painfully sensitive (place on the body)
sorely soreness sorer sorest

sorry
feeling regret or sorrow; miserable
sorrier sorriest

sort
group or kind with similar characteristics; to separate into different groups

sought
past tense and past participle of **seek**

soul
spiritual part of a human being; innermost part; person
soulful soulless

sound[1]
noise; to seem; to make a noise
soundless

sound[2]
healthy; undamaged; whole; deep
soundly

soup
liquid food made from meat, vegetables, etc.

sour
having an acid or vinegary taste; bad-tempered
sourly sourness

source
point of origin; starting-point of a river

south
one of the 4 compass points, opposite of north
south-east or southeast southerly southern southerner southward southwards south-west or southwest

souvenir
something that serves as a reminder of a person or place

sovereign
king or queen; supreme; former British gold coin worth 1 pound
sovereignty

sow[1]
to plant seed
sowed sower sowing sown

sow[2]
adult female pig

space
boundless expanse in which objects are located; area beyond earth's atmosphere; distance between objects; to place with spaces between
spacer spacing spacious

spade
tool for digging and lifting soil

span[1]
distance or space between 2 points, esp. the supports of a bridge or arch; period of time; to reach across
spanned spanning

span[2]
past tense of spin

spare
to manage to give or afford; to refrain from using, hurting, or punishing; additional; duplicate
sparely spareness sparing sparingly

spark
small burning particle thrown out from a fire; flash of light produced electrically; trace; to produce a spark

sparkle
to reflect flashes of light
sparkler sparkling

spat
past tense and past participle of **spit**[1]

speak
to utter or talk; to show
speaker speaking spoke spoken

special
not common; individual
or exceptional
specialist speciality specialities
specialize or *specialise*

species
(biological) group

specific
exact; particular
specifically specification specify

specimen
individual (typical) item

spectacular
very impressive

speculate
to conjecture; to risk money in the
hope of gaining profit
speculating speculation speculative
speculator

speech
faculty of speaking; public talk
speeches speechless

speed
rate at which something moves;
to move quickly
sped speeding speedometer

spell[1]
to say or write the letters of a word
in the correct way; words used as a
magic formula
spelled or *spelt speller spelling*

spell[2]
period of time

spend
to pay out money; to use up
or pass time
spender spending spent

sphere
round ball or globe; area or range
of knowledge, activities, etc.
spherical

spice
substance used as flavouring;
to flavour with spices
spicier spiciest spiciness spicing spicy

spider
8-legged creature that spins threads
of silk
spidery

spill
to (allow to) fall over; overflow
spilled or *spilt spilling*

spin
to draw out and twist into a thread;
to turn round and round fast; short
ride in a car, etc.
spinner spinning spun or span

spiral
winding round and round at an
increasing distance from the centre;
to move in this way
spiralled (US *spiraled*) *spiralling*
(US *spiraling*)

spirit
animating part of human beings;
ghost; enthusiasm; alcohol
spirited spiritless spiritual spiritualism
spiritualist spirituality spiritually

spit[1]
to eject saliva from the mouth;
(of rain) to fall lightly
spat spitter spitting

spit[2]
thin metal spike pushed into meat for roasting; long narrow projecting strip of land

spite
maliciousness; defiance;
to annoy out of spite
spiteful spitefully spiting

splash
to make wet with drops of water

splendid
brilliant; excellent
splendidly splendour
(US *splendor*)

split
to break or divide into parts;
act of splitting; division or part
splitting

spoil
to damage the value, usefulness, etc., of; to pamper
spoiled or *spoilt*

spoke
past tense of speak

spoken
past participle of speak

spokesman
(fem. **spokeswoman**)
representative speaker
spokesperson

sponge
kind of sea animal with a very porous body; skeleton of this, used for washing; to live at another person's expense
sponger sponging spongy

sponsor
person who supports or promotes a project
sponsorship

spoon
utensil with a shallow round bowl on a handle
spoonful

sport
game with physical activity,
played for entertainment or exercise;
to wear or show
sporting sporty

spot
small mark; drop; pimple;
to mark with spots
spotless spotted spotting spotty

spray
(to disperse) fine particles of a liquid;
single slender branch or shoot

spread
to unfold or extend; to apply

spring
to rise quickly and suddenly; (device that is able, when compressed) to return quickly to its original form;
season between winter and summer
sprang springy springier springiest sprung

spun
past tense and past participle of **spin**

spur
pointed device worn on a horserider's heel to urge on a horse; stimulus; projecting ridge; to urge on
spurred spurring

spy
person employed to discover secret information about a rival country or institution; to catch sight of
spies spied spying

squad
small group of people working together as a team

square
figure with 4 equal sides and 4 right angles; to multiply a number by itself; result of this; even

squat
to sit on one's heels; to occupy property illegally; dumpy
squatted squatter squatting

squeeze
to press tightly; to force through a narrow space;
act of squeezing
squeezer squeezing

stab
to pierce or wound with a sharp pointed instrument; instance of stabbing; attempt
stabbed stabbing

stable[1]
steady or firm
stability stabilize

stable[2]
shelter for horses;
to put in a stable
stabling

stadium
large sportsground or arena
stadium or *stadia*

staff
personnel or workers (pl. *staffs*); pole (pl. *staffs* or *staves*)

stage
raised platform in a theatre;
step or period of development;
to perform a play
staging

stain
to discolour, dye, or blemish; mark caused by staining

stair
one of a series of indoor steps from one level to another

stake
pointed piece of metal or wood used as a marker or support; to mark or support with a stake; money risked on the outcome of a race, etc.;
to risk money
staking

stale
not fresh; dull
staleness staler stalest

stall
booth from which business is transacted; compartment in a stable for an animal; seat in the ground floor of a theatre; (of an engine) to stop unintentionally

stamp
printed piece of paper to be stuck on letters to show that postage has been paid; to bring the foot down heavily; to print

stand
to take up and remain in an upright position; to endure; table for displaying goods; stall
standing stood

standard
flag; principle; level of quality, etc., by which things may be evaluated; accepted or conventional
standardize or *standardise*

stank
past tense of **stink**

star
heavenly body seen as a point of light at night; to mark with a star; to perform a leading role in
stardom starred starring starry

stare
to look at fixedly; such a look
stared staring

start
to begin; to make a sudden startled movement; beginning; lead
starter

startle
to surprise or shock
startling

starve
(to cause) to die from lack of food
starvation starving

state
condition; civil government; political community; to express or utter
stateless statement stating

station
stopping place for trains; local office of police; rank; to locate

stationary
not moving

stationery
writing materials
stationer

statistics
study of collecting, analysing, etc., data; presentation of data
statistical statistically statistician

statue
carved or moulded figure of a person or animal
statuary statuesque statuette

status
person's rank or standing

stay
to remain; to reside temporarily; period of staying
stayed staying

steady
(to make) stable; continuing at the same rate
steadier steadiest steadily steadiness

steak
thick slice of meat or fish

steal
to take the property of someone else illegally or without permission; to move furtively
stealing stole stolen

steam
vapour into which boiling water turns; to cook by this
steamer steamy

steel
hard alloy of iron and carbon
steely

steep
sloping sharply

steer
to guide the course of a vehicle
steering

stem
stalk of plant; main part of word; to arise (from); to stop the flow of
stemmed stemming

step
surface for the foot when going up or down; to move the foot by raising it and setting it down; action or stage in a process
stepped stepping

stereo
(sound system) using 2 channels
stereos stereophonic

stick[1]
long narrow piece of wood

stick[2]
to attach by using an adhesive, etc.; to become fixed
sticker sticky stuck

stiff
rigid; not flexible; formal; difficult
stiffen

still
not moving; not effervescent; to make still; nevertheless; even
stillness

stimulus
something that arouses or excites; incentive
stimuli stimulant stimulate stimulating stimulation

sting
to inflict a wound or to inject poison; act of stinging; organ that stings
stung

stink
(to emit a) strong offensive smell
stank or *stunk stinker stinking*

stir
to move slightly; to mix with a turning movement; commotion
stirred stirrer stirring

stitch
(to make a) complete loop made by a needle and thread; sudden sharp pain in the side
stitches

stock
(to) supply or store; farm animals; money lent to a government; liquid in which meat, etc., has simmered
stockist

stocking
close-fitting covering for a woman's leg and foot
stockinged

stole
past tense of steal

stolen
past participle of steal

stomach
bag-like part of the body into which food passes after it has been swallowed; abdomen; to tolerate

stone
(small piece of) rock; to throw stones at; (to remove the) hard covering round the seed of some plants; unit of weight, 14 pounds
stonier stoniest stonily stoniness stoning stony

stood
past tense and past participle of stand

stool
seat without a back or arms; discharge from the bowels

stop
to bring or come to a halt; to prevent; to block or suppress; state of being stopped; place where buses, etc., stop
stoppage stopped stopper stopping

storage
(space available for) storing something

store
to keep for future use; supply; shop; storage place
storing

storey (US **story**)
floor or level of a building
storeyed storeys (US *stories*)

storm
burst of violent weather; (to) attack violently
stormier stormiest stormily storminess stormy

story
account of events; (US) storey
stories

stove
cooking or heating apparatus

straight
(part that is) not curved; correct or honest; directly
straighten

strain
to tighten; to exert oneself to the limit; to filter; stress
strainer

strange
peculiar; unfamiliar
strangely strangeness stranger strangest

stranger
person who is unfamiliar to one

strap
(to secure with a) long strip of leather or other flexible material
strapped strapping

strategy
art of planning operations or campaigns
strategies strategic strategically strategist

straw
stalks of threshed grain; narrow drinking tube

strawberry
kind of (plant bearing) juicy red fruit
strawberries

stream
small river; to move in a steady flow; to group according to ability

street
road in a town

strength
state or quality of being strong
strengthen

stress
emphasis; to emphasize; tension
stresses stressful

stretch
to make wider or longer by pulling; to extend; continuous expanse or extent
stretches stretchable stretchy

strict
demanding obedience; severe; precise
strictly strictness

stride
long step; to walk with long steps
striding strode

strike
to hit; to inflict a blow; to produce a sound; to stop work because of a grievance; stoppage of work because of a grievance
striker striking struck

string
thin length of cord; tightly stretched wire on a musical instrument; to provide with strings
stringy strung

strip
long narrow piece; to remove the covering of
stripped stripper stripping

stripe
band of a different colour, texture, etc.
striped stripy

stroke[1]
to pass the hand gently over
stroking

stroke[2]
blow or movement; striking of a ball; sudden attack, esp. causing paralysis

strong
having strength or power; robust, not fragile; alcoholic

struck
past tense and past participle of **strike**

structure
construction, arrangement, or framework; building
structural structurally

struggle
to make great efforts; (to) fight; great effort
struggling

strung
past tense and past participle of **string**

stubborn
obstinate
stubbornly stubbornness

stuck
past tense and past participle of **stick**

student
person who studies

studio
room in which radio or television programmes are made; workroom of an artist or photographer
studios

study
to use the mind in order to gain knowledge of; to examine closely; room for studying
studies studied studious studying

stuff
to pack tightly; material or substance
stuffing

stun
to overwhelm; to make unconscious
stunned stunner stunning

stung
past tense and past participle of **sting**

stunk
past participle of **stink**

stupid
foolish; unthinking; dazed
stupefy stupidity stupidly stupor

style
manner; form or appearance; elegance; to shape
styling stylish stylist stylistic stylistically stylize or *stylise*

subconscious
part of the mind involved in mental activities of which one is not aware
subconsciously

subdue
to control or overcome; to make less intense
subdued subduing

subject
branch of study; topic being discussed; word or phrase in a sentence about which something is said; to conquer; to cause to undergo
subjection

subjective
not objective; personal
subjectively subjectivity

submarine
(vessel, esp. a warship, designed to travel) under the sea

submerge
to place under water; to sink
submerging submersible

submit
to yield; to present for consideration
submission submissive submitted submitting

subscribe
to pay money regularly to an organization providing a magazine, etc.
subscriber subscribing subscription

subsequent
following
subsequently

subsidy
money paid by a government, as to an industry in financial difficulty
subsidies subsidize or *subsidise*

substance
(solid) matter; essential part
substantial substantially

substitute
(to use a) person or thing to replace another
substituting substitution

subtle
not easily detectable; indirect; delicate
subtler subtlest subtlety subtleties subtly

subtract
to take away one number or quantity from another
subtraction

suburb
residential district on the outskirts of a city or town
suburban suburbia

succeed
to achieve an aim; to inherit; to follow
succession successive successor

success
achievement of an aim

successful
achieving the intended aim
successfully

such
of the same or that kind; so great or intense; mentioned before
suchlike

suck
to draw a liquid into the mouth
sucker suction

sudden
quickly and unexpectedly
suddenly suddenness

suffer
to experience pain, etc.; (formal) to tolerate
sufferance sufferer suffering

sufficient
adequate
suffice sufficing sufficiency sufficiently

sugar
sweet substance obtained from sucrose; to add sugar to
sugary

suggest
to present for consideration; to cause one to think
suggestion suggestive

suicide
deliberate killing of oneself; person who dies in this way
suicidal suicidally

suit
set of outer clothes; set of playing-cards; legal case; to be appropriate for

suitable
appropriate or fitting
suitability suitably

suitcase
portable travelling case for clothes, etc.

suite
set of rooms; matching set of furniture; musical composition

sum
total amount; simple arithmetical problem;
to summarize
summed summing

summary
concise statement of facts; performed without delay
summaries summarize or *summarise*

summer
season between spring and autumn
summery

summit
top of a mountain; meeting of heads of governments

sun
star around which the earth and other planets revolve
sunnier sunniest sunny

Sunday
1st day of the week

sung
past participle of sing

sunk
past participle of sink

sunset
time when the sun disappears below the horizon

sunshine
light from the sun

super
(informal) excellent

superb
excellent

superior
(person who is) higher in rank or worth
superiority

supermarket
large self-service shop

supersede
to take the place of
superseding

supervise
to be in charge of or direct work or workers
supervising supervision supervisor supervisory

supper
evening meal or snack

supplement
(to make an) addition
supplementary supplementation

supply
to provide with; something provided; store
supplies supplied supplier supplying

support
to bear the weight of; to give aid to; to back; structure that supports
supporter supporting supportive

suppose
to believe to be true;
to necessitate
supposed supposedly supposing supposition

suppress
to prohibit or restrain
suppresses suppression

supreme
highest (in authority, etc.)
supremacy supremely

sure
certain or confident
surely surer surest

surface
external area or top of something; to rise to the surface
surfacing

surgery
treatment of diseases by operations; place where a doctor or dentist treats patients
surgeries surgeon surgical surgically

surname
family name

surprise
to amaze suddenly; to startle; something unexpected
surprised surprising surprisingly

surrender
to yield control over; to give (oneself) up

surround
to enclose on all sides; border
surroundings

survey
to view; to examine or inspect; to measure and plot land; view; examination or report
surveying surveyor

survive
to continue to live (through)
survival surviving survivor

suspect
to have doubts about; to consider likely; to believe to be guilty of a crime; person who may be guilty of a crime; arousing suspicion

suspend
to hang; to postpone; to keep immobile in a liquid or air
suspender suspension

suspense
feeling of tense waiting

suspicion
doubt; feeling that something is likely
suspicious suspiciously

sustain
to maintain; to support; to undergo
sustainable sustenance

swallow[1]
to send food, etc., down the throat into the stomach

swallow[2]
fork-tailed migratory bird

swam
past tense of **swim**

swan
kind of large long-necked water bird; (informal) to wander aimlessly (about)
swanned swanning

swap or **swop**
(informal) to exchange
swapped or *swopped swapping* or *swopping*

sway
to (cause to) swing gently from side to side; (to) influence

a b c d e f g h i j k l m n o p q r s t u v w x y z

swear
to promise or assert on oath or emphatically; to use bad language
swearer swearing swore sworn

sweat
(to exude) moisture passed out of the body through the pores
sweaty

sweater
pullover

sweep
to clean or clear away with a brush; to move or pass quickly
sweeper sweeping swept

sweet
tasting of or like sugar; fresh; piece of confectionery; dessert
sweeten sweetener

swell
to expand; to bulge
swelled swelling swollen

swift
fast; kind of long-winged bird that has a fast darting flight

swim
to move the body through water; to have a dizzy feeling
swam swimmer swimming swum

swing
to move to and fro, hanging freely; child's suspended seat that swings
swung

switch
(to turn on or off using a) device that operates an electric current; to shift
switches

swop
see **swap**

sword
weapon with long blade

swore
past tense of **swear**

sworn
past participle of **swear**

swum
past participle of **swim**

syllable
unit of a word that contains a vowel
syllabification

symbol
sign that represents something
symbolic symbolically symbolism

sympathy
ability to share another person's feelings;
feeling of compassion
sympathies sympathetic sympathetically sympathize or *sympathise*

symptom
sign, esp. of a disease
symptomatic

synagogue
place of Jewish worship

system
combination of related parts; ordered scheme
systematic systematically systematize or *systematise*

Tt

table
flat-topped piece of furniture; orderly arrangement of data; to present for discussion
tabling

tablet
small flat slab; small compressed piece; pill

tackle
arrangement of ropes and pulleys for lifting things; to deal with; to try and take the ball from
tackling

tact
skill in dealing with people without causing offence
tactful tactfully tactless

tactic
plan for achieving an aim
tactical tactically tactics tactician

tail
movable part that extends from the back of an animal; to follow closely

tailor
person who makes men's clothes; to adjust or adapt

take
to hold or seize; to obtain; to carry; to steal
takeover taking took

tale
story; lie or gossip

talent
natural ability or skill
talented

talk
to speak; conversation; lecture
talkative talker

tall
of greater than average height
taller tallest

tame
not wild; to bring under human control
tameable or *tamable tamely tameness tamer tamest taming*

tan
to turn animal skin into leather; to turn brown from exposure to the sun; yellowish-brown
tanned tanner tanning

tangle
confused mass or state; to make or become confused or untidy
tangled tangling

tank
large container for liquids or gases; heavily armoured military vehicle
tanker tankful

tap[1]
to strike gently
tapped tapping

tap[2]
valve for controlling the flow of a gas or liquid; to draw from;
to connect a listening device to a telephone line in order to gain secret information
tapped tapping

tape
long narrow strip of material; long narrow strip of plastic with a coating that can be magnetized, used to record sound, video, etc.; to record on to magnetic tape
taping

target
object or aim, esp. for shooting at;
to make a target of
targeted targeting

tariff
tax on goods imported or exported;
list of prices

task
piece of work; duty

taste
sense by which flavour is perceived;
to recognize or have the flavour of;
ability to appreciate aesthetically fine matters
tasteful tastefully tasteless tastier tastiest tastiness tasting tasty

taught
past tense and past participle of **teach**

tax
sum of money levied by a government on income, etc.;
to levy a tax on; to make demands of
taxes taxable taxation taxing

taxi
car that may be hired with a driver;
(of an aircraft) to move along the ground
taxis taxied taxies taxiing

tea
(drink made from) the dried leaves of an evergreen Asian shrub;
late-afternoon or early-evening meal

teach
to give instruction to or in
taught teachable teacher teaches teaching

team
group of people organized to work or play together

tear[1]
drop of liquid coming from the eye
tearful tearfully

tear[2]
to pull apart forcefully;
to make a hole in something;
(to) rip
tore torn

tease
to make fun of; to annoy;
to untangle with a comb;
to raise the nap on
teaser teasing

technical
of or concerned with industrial or applied sciences
technicality technicalities technically technician

technique
method of doing something skilfully

technology
application of science to industry and commerce
technologies technological technologically technologist

teenage
of a person aged from 13 to 19
teenaged teenager

teeth
pl. of **tooth**

telephone
(to use an) electrical device for speaking and listening to someone at a distance
telephonic telephonically telephoning telephonist

telescope
optical instrument used to view distant objects; to become shorter or crushed
telescopic telescoping

television
system that transmits images and sound over a distance; apparatus that receives these images
televise televising

tell
to inform or relate
teller telling told

temper
mood; angry state; to harden a metal; to moderate

temperament
person's character and disposition
temperamental temperamentally

temperature
level of heat

temple
building dedicated to the worship of a god; flat area on either side of the forehead

temporary
lasting only for a limited time
temporarily temporariness

tempt
to entice or attempt to persuade to do something
temptation tempter tempting temptress

ten
number 10
tenner tenth

tenant
person who rents land or property
tenancy tenancies

tend[1]
to look after

tend[2]
to be inclined to

tendency
inclination; general trend
tendencies

tender
not tough; delicate or sensitive; loving

tennis
ball-game for 2 or 4 people who hit a ball with rackets over a net

tense[1]
tightly stretched; worried, esp. about what is going to happen; to make or become tense
tensely tenseness tenser tensest tensing

tense[2]
(grammar) verb form expressing time distinctions

tension
(degree of) tenseness; mental or emotional strain

tent
collapsible shelter supported by poles

term
expression; period of time; division of academic year

terminal
at the end; (of a disease) ending in death; terminus; airport building
terminally

terrace
level area of ground; row of houses; tier around sportsground
terraced

terrible
(informal) very bad; extreme; terrifying
terribly

terrific
(informal) very good; intense
terrifically

terrify
to fill with terror
terrified terrifies terrifying

territory
land; region of a country
territories territorial territorially

terror
great fear; (informal) troublesome person
terrorize or *terrorise*

terrorism
use of violence and intimidation to achieve esp. political goals
terrorist

test
to examine; to try (out); examination

text
written matter, as opposed to illustrations; to send a text message
textual

textile
woven or knitted cloth

texture
surface characteristics of something as perceived by touch or sight; special quality
textural textured

than
word used in comparisons

thank
to express gratitude to
thankful thankfully thankless

thanks
word used to express gratitude; owing (to)

that
person or thing referred to; opposite of **this**; used to introduce a clause
that'll that's

the
definite article

theatre (US **theater**)
place where plays are performed publicly; hospital room where surgical operations are carried out
theatrical theatrically

theft
stealing

their
possessive form of **they**

theirs
(the one or ones) belonging to *them*

them
object form of **they**

theme
topic; main musical melody
thematic thematically

themselves
reflexive form of **they**

then
at that time; next

theory
set of explanatory ideas; principles of a subject
theories theoretical theoretically theorist theorize or *theorise*

there
in or to that place; used to introduce a sentence

therefore
for that reason

thermometer
instrument used to measure temperature

these
pl. of **this**

they
people or things mentioned; people in general
they'd they'll they're they've

thick
not thin; dense; (informal) stupid
thicken thicker thickest thickly thickness

thief
person who steals
thieves thievish

thigh
part of the leg between the hip and the knee

thin
narrow; slender; not thick; to make or become thin
thinly thinned thinner thinness thinnest thinning

thing
object, event, or circumstance

think
to consider; to have as an opinion
thinkable thinker thinking thought

third
coming next after second

thirst
(to feel a) great longing for a drink
thirstier thirstiest thirstily thirsty

thirteen
number 13
thirteenth

thirty
number 30
thirties thirtieth

this
person or thing that is near; opposite of **that**; to such an extent
this'll

thorn
sharp-pointed prickle on a plant
thornier thorniest thorny

thorough
careful; complete
thoroughly thoroughness

those
pl. of **that**

though
although; however

thought
past tense and past participle of **think**; result or act of thinking
thoughtful thoughtfully thoughtless thoughtlessly

thousand
number 1000
thousandth

thread
strand of material, esp. cotton; to pass a thread through a needle

threat
intention to injure or punish; sign of something unpleasant

threaten
to be or express a threat to
threateningly

three
number 3
three-quarters

threshold
piece of wood or stone below a doorway; beginning

threw
past tense of **throw**

thrill
(to (cause to) feel a) sudden sensation of pleasurable excitement
thriller thrilling thrillingly

throat
front of the neck; passage in the neck through which food passes
throatier throatiest throaty

throne
ceremonial seat of a sovereign or a bishop

through
in on one side and out on the other; from the beginning to the end of; as a result of

throughout
in every part of; for the whole duration of

throw
to send forcefully through the air; to shape on a potter's wheel
threw thrown

thrust
(to give a) violent push

thumb
short thick finger that is at an angle to the other fingers; to turn pages with the thumb

thump
(to strike with a) heavy solid blow

thunder
loud noise following a flash of lightning; to sound with or like thunder
thunderous thundery

Thursday
5th day of the week

thus
in this way; therefore

ticket
printed card showing that the holder has certain rights, for example to travel; label;
to issue tickets to
ticketed ticketing

tide
regular rise and fall of the level of the sea; to help a person live through a difficult period
tidal tiding

tidy
(to make) neat and orderly
tidied tidier tidies tidiest tidily tidiness tidying

tie
to fasten or attach; piece of cloth worn round the neck;
(to make an) equal score
ties tied tying

tiger (fem. **tigress**)
large tawny animal of the cat family with black stripes

tight
fully stretched; packed closely; not loose
tighter tightest tightly tightness

tile
(to cover with a) thin slab of baked clay, linoleum, etc.
tiling

till[1]
until

till[2]
cash register; container for money in a shop

timber
wood that is suitable for carpentry or building
timbered timbering

time
period during which or point at which something happens; continuous passage of existence; point in time shown in hours, minutes, etc.;
to measure the duration of
timed timeless timely timer timing

timetable
chart showing times of arrival and departure of trains or buses;
(to) schedule
timetabling

tin
(to cover with a) soft silvery-white metal; (to preserve in a) container made of tin-plate
tinned tinning tinny

tiny
very small
tinier tiniest tininess

tip[1]
end of something; to mark the end of something; to hit or touch lightly
tipped tipping

tip[2]
to tilt or overturn
tipped tipping

tip[2]
(to give a) sum of money for service; piece of advice or information
tipped tipping

tire
to make or become tired
tireless tirelessly tiresome tiring

tired
lacking energy and ready to rest
tiredly tiredness

tissue
thin paper handkerchief; fine cloth; mass of cells or fibres that make up a structure in the body

title
name of a book, etc.; word that shows rank or status; proof of ownership, right or rank
titled titular

to
in the direction of; as far as; before the hour of

toast
to make bread crisp and brown by heating; toasted bread; (to) drink to someone's health, etc.
toaster

tobacco
plant, the leaves of which are used to make cigarettes, cigars, etc.
tobaccos tobacconist

today
on this day; at the present time

toe
(to touch with) one of the 5 digits of the foot
toed toeing

together
with each other; into contact
together

toilet
(room containing a) fixture for receiving and disposing of urine and faeces; act of washing and preparing oneself
toiletries

told
past tense and past participle of **tell**

tolerate
to allow or endure
tolerable tolerably tolerance tolerant tolerantly tolerating toleration

toll[1]
(of a bell) to (cause to) ring slowly and regularly
tolled tolling

toll[2]
tax levied for the use of a road, bridge, etc.

tomato
kind of (plant with) red fleshy fruit
tomatoes

tomb
structure in which a corpse is laid to rest

tomorrow
day after today

ton
unit of weight

tone
(quality of) sound; shade of colour; musical interval of 2 semitones; to give a tone to
tonal tonality toned toner toning

tongue
movable organ in the mouth; power of speech; language; to touch with the tongue
tongued tongueing

tonight
during the evening or night of the present day

tonne
unit of weight, metric ton, 1000 kilograms

too
excessively; as well

took
past tense of take

tool
implement, esp. one that is held in the hand

tooth
hard bony structure in the mouth used for biting, chewing, etc.
teeth toothed toothless toothsome toothy

top
highest part of something; to cover; to exceed
topless topmost topped topping

topic
subject or theme

topical
of current interest
topicality

torch
portable electric light powered by batteries
torches

tore
past tense of **tear**[2]

torn
past participle of **tear**[2]

tortoise
slow-moving reptile with a hard dome-shaped shell

torture
to inflict intense pain on, esp. to obtain information from; infliction of such pain
tortured torturer torturing

toss
to throw; to move about restlessly; tossing action
tosses

total
whole amount; whole or complete; to add up the total
totality totalled (US *totaled*) *totalling* (US *totaling*) *totally*

touch
to feel or handle; to come into contact with; to move emotionally; sense of feeling
touches touchable touched touchier touchiest touching touchy

tough
difficult to tear, cut, or chew; determined; strong
toughen tougher toughest toughness

tour
(to make a) journey in which several visits are made
touring

tourist
person who travels for pleasure
tourism touristy

tournament
series of sporting games

tow
to pull or drag with a rope, etc.

towards or **toward**
in the direction of

towel
absorbent cloth for drying or wiping after washing; to use a towel
towelled (US *toweled*) *towelling* (US *toweling*)

tower
tall structure; to rise to a great height
towering

town
densely populated area larger than a village but smaller than a city

toy
object designed to be played with; to treat or handle casually
toys toyed toying

trace
mark left by something; slight indication; to follow the course of; to copy the outline of through thin paper
traceable tracer tracing

track
trail or series of marks made by the passage of a person, animal, etc.; rough path; rails for a train, tram, etc., to run on; to follow the track of

trade
(to engage in the) buying and selling of goods; business
tradable or *tradeable trader tradesman trading*

tradition
passing down of belief, custom, etc., from one generation to another; belief, custom, etc., passed down in this way
traditional traditionalist traditionally

traffic
flow of vehicles; to trade in illegal goods
trafficked trafficker trafficking

tragedy
calamity or disaster; drama with an unhappy ending
tragedies tragedian tragic tragically

trail
(to follow a) mark or track left by a person or thing; to drag behind one
trailer

train
set of coaches or wagons connected to a railway engine; to teach a particular skill to
trainee trainer training

traitor (fem. **traitress**)
person who acts disloyally or commits treason
traitorous

tranquil
calm; peaceful
tranquillity tranquillize or *tranquillise tranquillizer* or *tranquilliser tranquilly*

transfer
to move from one place to another; to convey the ownership of to another person; to move a design from one surface to another; to move a design in this way
transferable transferee transference transferred transferring

transform
to change the form, nature, etc., of
transformable transformation transformer

transition
development from one stage or condition to another
transitional

translate
to express in another language
translatable translating translation translator

transmit
to send a signal, etc.; to transfer or pass on
transmissible or *transmittable transmission transmitted transmitter transmitting*

transparent
allowing the uninterrupted passage of light
transparency

transplant
to transfer a plant to another position; to transfer an organ into another body; something transplanted
transplantation

transport
to convey from one place to another; means of transporting
transportable transportation transporter

trap
device for catching animals; device or ruse to trick a person; to catch in a trap; light 2-wheeled carriage
trapped trapper trapping

trauma
powerful and deep shock
traumas or *traumata traumatic traumatically traumatize* or *traumatise*

travel
to make a journey; to move
travelled (US *traveled*) *traveller* (US *traveler*) *travelling* (US *traveling*)

tray
open receptacle with a low rim for carrying articles

tread
to step or walk; to crush; external surface of a tyre
treading trod trodden

treasure
very valuable object; wealth; to value highly
treasured treasurer treasuring treasury

treat
to deal with or act towards; to care for medically; entertainment paid for by others
treatable treatment

treaty
formal agreement between countries
treaties

tree
large perennial woody plant with a trunk and branches

tremble
to shake or quiver; trembling movement
trembling trembly

tremendous
great; (informal) very good

trend
(to show a) general tendency
trendier trendiest trendiness trendsetter trendsetting trendy

trial
legal examination to determine a person's guilt or innocence

triangle
3-sided geometric figure; triangular percussion instrument
triangular triangulate triangulation

tribe
very large social group
tribal tribalism tribesman

tribute
something given or said as an expression of thanks, respect, etc.

trick
cunning or mischievous action; to deceive or cheat; cards played in 1 round of a card-game
trickery trickier trickiest trickily trickiness trickster tricky

tried
past tense and past participle of **try**

trifle
something of little value; dessert made with sponge, jelly, custard, etc.; to deal carelessly (with)
trifler trifling

trigger
lever that releases the firing mechanism of a gun; to set (off)

trim
neat and tidy; to clip; physical condition
trimly trimmed trimmer trimmest trimming

trip
to (cause to) stumble; journey; (informal) experience resulting from drug-taking
tripped tripper tripping

triple
having 3 parts; (to make or become) 3 times as large
triplicate tripling triply

triumph
(to win a) victory or success
triumphal triumphant triumphantly

trivial
unimportant
triviality trivialize or *trivialise*

trod
past tense of **tread**

trodden
past participle of **tread**

trolley
basket on wheels for carrying goods; small truck; small table on castors
trolleys

troop
military unit; (to move as a) large group

trophy
prize; memento of success
trophies

tropical
coming from or located in the area between the tropic of Cancer and the tropic of Capricorn; (informal) very hot

trot
(of horses) (to move at a) speed that is faster than a walk but slower than a canter
trotted trotting

trouble
(cause of) difficulty; to cause trouble; (to make an) effort
troublesome troubling

trousers
2-legged garment covering the body from the waist to the ankles

truck
railway wagon; (chiefly US) lorry
trucker trucking

true
not false; real; exact; faithful; accurate alignment
truer truest truly

trumpet
(to blow a) valved brass musical instrument
trumpeted trumpeter trumpeting

trunk
main stem of a tree; large strong box with a hinged lid; human body excluding head and limbs; elephant's snout; (US) car boot

trust
(to have a) firm belief or confidence in; responsibility
trustee trusteeship trustful trusting trustingly trustworthiness trustworthy trusty

truth
quality of being true; something that is true

truthful
telling the truth; accurate
truthfully truthfulness

try
(to) attempt; to examine or test; to investigate in a law-court; (rugby) touchdown behind the opponent's goal line
tries tried trier trying

tube
hollow cylinder; (Brit) London underground railway
tubed tubeless tubing tubular

Tuesday
3rd day of the week

tug
to pull hard; powerful boat for towing ships
tugged tugging

tumour (US **tumor**)
abnormal swelling

tune
melody; (to put into) standard pitch; to adjust a radio or television set to receive a signal; to adjust an engine to give the best performance
tuneable or *tunable tuneful tunefully tuneless tuner tuning*

tunnel
(to dig an) underground passageway
tunnelled (US *tunneled*) *tunnelling* (US *tunneling*)

turkey
kind of large bird farmed for its meat
turkeys

turn
to (cause to) move round; to (cause to) change position or direction; to shape on a lathe; turning action; opportunity or right to do something

turning
road that leads off another

turnover
value of goods and services sold; rate at which staff, etc., are replaced; small pie

tutor
private teacher; university teacher; to act as a tutor to
tutorial tutorially

twelve
number 12
twelfth

twenty
number 20
twenties twentieth

twice
2 times

twig
small branch or shoot of a tree

twilight
soft dim light between sunset and full darkness
twilit

twin
either of 2 offspring born at the same birth; similar or related; to pair
twinned twinning

twist
to wind strands together to form a thread; to wind; twisting movement
twister twisty

two
number 2

type
class or group that share similar characteristics; to write with or use a typewriter; set of blocks used in printing
typing typist

typewriter
machine with a keyboard for producing letters and figures resembling printed ones
typewrite typewriting typewritten typewrote

typical
having the main characteristics of
typically

typify
to be typical of; to characterize or symbolize
typified typifies typifying

tyrant
oppressive and unjust ruler
tyrannical tyrannically tyrannize or *tyrannise tyrannous tyranny tyrannies*

tyre (US **tire**)
rubber ring set round a wheel

Section Notes

Section Notes

Uu

ugly
unpleasant to look at; menacing
uglier ugliest ugliness

ultimate
final; fundamental
ultimately

ultimatum
final demand
ultimatums or *ultimata*

umbrella
portable device that gives protection from the weather

umpire
(to) referee in a sport such as tennis or cricket; judge
umpiring

unable
not able

unanimous
agreeing; marked by complete agreement
unanimity unanimously

unaware
not aware
unawares

uncanny
mysterious; extraordinary
uncannily

uncertain
not certain; not to be relied on
uncertainty

uncle
brother of one's father or mother; aunt's husband

uncomfortable
not comfortable; feeling nervous or embarrassed
uncomfortably

unconscious
not aware; not conscious; unconscious mind
unconsciously unconsciousness

uncover
to remove the cover from; to disclose

under
below; less than

underclothes
underwear
underclothing

underdone
not fully cooked

underestimate
to make too low an estimate of
underestimating underestimation

undergo
to experience; to be subjected to
undergoing undergone underwent

undergraduate
person studying for a first degree

underground
beneath the earth's surface; secretly or secret; underground railway

underline
to draw a line under; to emphasize
underlining

underlying
forming the basis of; lying beneath

undermine
to tunnel under; to weaken
undermining

underneath
below or beneath

understand
to realize the meaning of; to have a thorough knowledge of; to believe; to sympathize
understandable understandably understood

understanding
ability to understand; informal agreement; knowledge; sympathy

undertake
to take a task upon oneself; to promise
undertaken undertaking undertook

undertaker
person whose business is to arrange the dead for burial and to arrange funerals

underwater
beneath the surface of water, esp. the sea

underwear
garments worn next to the skin under other clothing

undo
to untie or unfasten; to ruin; to reverse the effect of
undid undoing undone

undress
to remove the clothes of; state of having too few clothes on; ordinary dress, not ceremonial uniform

uneasy
awkward
uneasily uneasiness

unemployed
(people who are) out of work; not being used
unemployment

unfair
not fair
unfairly

unfit
unsuitable; incapable; unwell; to make unfit
unfitted unfitting

unfortunate
unlucky; regrettable; unfortunate person
unfortunately

unhappy
sad; unfortunate
unhappier unhappiest unhappily unhappiness

uniform
identifying clothing worn by members of a particular group; unchanging
uniformed uniformity uniformly

unify
to make separate units into one
unification unified unifies unifying

union
uniting; group of workers formed to advance members' interests
unionism unionist unionize or *unionise*

unique
being the only one of its kind
uniquely uniqueness

unit
single person, thing, or group; part having a particular function
unitary

unite
to join; to become one
united uniting

unity
state of being united

universal
of or affecting all; existing everywhere
universality universalize or *universalise universally*

universe
all things that exist; everyone

university
higher educational institution for teaching and research
universities

unkempt
untidy or dishevelled

unkind
mean, spiteful, or cruel
unkindly unkindness

unknown
not known (person, thing, etc.)

unless
if not

unlike
different from

unlikely
not probable
unlikelihood

unlock
to open with a key

unnecessary
not necessary
unnecessarily

unpleasant
not pleasant; distressing; rude or unkind
unpleasantness

unreasonable
not governed by reason; excessive
unreasonably

unruly
difficult to control
unrulier unruliest unruliness

untidy
not tidy
untidier untidiest untidily untidiness

until
up to the time that

unusual
strange
unusually

unwieldy
awkward to handle
unwieldily unwieldiness

unwilling
not willing
unwillingly

up
from a lower to a higher position, level, etc.; to an upright position; to act suddenly; to increase
upped upping

upbringing
education and training

update
to bring up to date
updating

uphill
towards the top of a slope

uphold
to support or maintain
upheld upholding

upholster
to fit a soft covering, springs, etc., to a piece of furniture
upholsterer upholstery

upkeep
maintenance of something in good condition; money needed for this

upon
on

upper
higher; part of a shoe or boot above the sole
uppermost

upright
vertical; honest; honourable; vertical support

upset
to turn over; to disturb; disturbance
upsetting

upside
down turned over completely; in confusion

upstairs
on or to a higher floor in a building

upwards
towards a higher level or position
upward

urban
of or resembling a city or town

urge
to drive on; to plead; strong drive
urging

urgent
requiring immediate attention
urgency urgently

us
object form of **we**

use
to put into action or service; to apply or consume; exploitation
usable or *useable usage user using*

used
already used; accustomed (to); having done or experienced something in the past

useful
able to be used practically; commendable
usefully usefulness

useless
having no practical use; weak; futile
uselessly uselessness

usual
normal or customary
usually

utility
usefulness; public service
utilities utilitarian utilize or *utilise*

utter[1]
to express
utterance

utter[2]
absolute
utterly

Section Notes

Vv

vacant
empty; not in use or occupied; marked by a lack of thought
vacancy vacancies vacate

vacation
holiday; making vacant

vaccinate
to inoculate with a vaccine
vaccinating vaccination

vaccine
preparation designed to produce immunity to a disease

vacuum
space that contains no matter
vacuums or *vacua*

vague
not clear; imprecise
vaguely vagueness vaguer vaguest

vain
excessively proud of one's appearance; futile
vainly vanity

valid
legally effective; justifiable
validate validity

valley
hollow in the earth's surface, esp. between hills or mountains

valuable
(something) having great monetary value

value
(to estimate the) amount of money thought to be equivalent to something; (to estimate the) importance (of); to esteem
valuation valued valueless valuer valuing

valve
device for controlling the flow of a liquid or gas

van
covered motor vehicle or railway wagon for transporting goods

vanish
to disappear
vanishes

variable
liable to vary
variability variably

variation
varying; slightly different version of something

variety
quality of being different; range of different kinds; group
varieties

various
several; different

vary
to change
variance variant varied varies varying

vase
ornamental container for flowers

vast
very large or wide
vastly vastness

vegetable
plant with a part used as food; this part

vegetarian
person who has a diet that excludes meat
vegetarianism

vehicle
means of conveying passengers or goods, esp. one fitted with wheels
vehicular

veil
light fabric worn by a woman to hide or protect the face or head; something that conceals; to cover with a veil

vein
thin-walled blood-vessel; streak of colour
veined venous

velvet
fabric of silk, cotton, etc., with a soft thick pile

venture
to risk; risky undertaking
venturing

verb
word expressing performance of an action, etc.

verbal
in words; spoken; of verbs
verbalize or *verbalise verbally*

verdict
decision, esp. one reached by a court

versatile
able to be used in many different ways
versatility

verse
group of lines in a poem or song; poetry
versify

version
account or description from a particular point of view

versus
against

vertical
upright
vertically

very
to a high degree; actual

vessel
container for liquids; ship or boat

vet
to assess or examine thoroughly; (*informal*) short for **veterinary surgeon**
vetted vetting

veterinary
of a branch of medicine concerned with the health and treatment of animals

veto
authority to forbid; act of forbidding; to forbid
vetoes vetoed vetoing

via
by way of

vice[1]
(form of) wickedness

vice[2] (US **vise**)
tool with 2 jaws for gripping an object

vice versa
the other way around

vicious
cruel or wicked
viciously viciousness

victim
person or thing that suffers harm or is tricked
victimize or *victimise*

victory
success or winning
victories victor victorious victoriously

video
recording of sound and vision on magnetic tape
videos

view
to watch or inspect; scene; opinion
viewer

vigour (US **vigor**)
strength or energy
vigorous vigorously

village
group of houses in a country area
villager

violent
forceful
violence violently

violet
kind of plant with sweet-scented bluish-purple flowers; bluish-purple colour

violin
kind of stringed musical instrument played with a bow
violinist

virtual
in effect though not in fact
virtually

virtue
goodness; chastity; advantageous quality
virtuous virtuously

virus
tiny organism that causes a disease; (*informal*) disease caused by this; small piece of software that upsets the normal running of a computer
viruses viral

visible
capable of being seen
visibility visibly

vision
power of seeing; vivid mental image; foresight
visionary visionaries

visit
to go to see; act of visiting
visitation visited visiting visitor

visual
of or associated with seeing
visualize or *visualise visually*

vital
of or concerned with living; essential
vitally

vitality
liveliness; vigour; energy

vitamin
organic compound essential for healthy life and growth

vivacious
lively
vivaciously vivacity

vivid
(of a colour) bright; strong or lively
vividly vividness

vocabulary
(alphabetical) list of words; set of words that are used
vocabularies

vocal
of or produced by the voice
vocalist vocalize or *vocalise vocally*

vocation
(sense of calling to follow a) particular profession
vocational vocationally

voice
sound produced from the mouth in speaking or singing; to express one's opinion, etc.
voicing

volcano
opening in the earth's crust from which lava, steam, etc., may be forced out
volcanoes or *volcanos volcanic*

volume
book, esp. one of a series; amount of space, loudness of sound
voluminous voluminously

voluntary
of one's own free choice; organ solo
voluntaries voluntarily

volunteer
to offer (oneself) freely; person who volunteers

vomit
to eject stomach contents through the mouth; matter that is vomited
vomited vomiting

vote
to express one's choice or opinion formally; formal expression of opinion
voter voting

vow
(to make a) solemn promise

vowel
speech sound or letter of the alphabet that is not a consonant

voyage
(to make a) long journey by sea or into space
voyager voyaging

vulnerable
capable of being hurt or wounded
vulnerability vulnerably

Ww

wage
payment for work, esp. paid weekly; to engage in war
wages waged waging

wager
(to make a) bet

wagon or **waggon**
open railway goods truck; 4-wheeled vehicle used for carrying heavy loads

waist
narrow part of the body between the ribs and hips

wait
to remain, expecting; to delay; to serve at table
waiter waitress

wake[1]
to rouse or become roused from sleep; to make or become conscious of; vigil by a corpse before burial; annual holiday in northern England
wakeful wakefully wakefulness waking woke woken

wake[2]
track or trail left by something moving, esp. through water

walk
to move on foot; journey on foot; calling or occupation
walker walking

wall
(to protect, etc., with a) solid vertical construction of stone, brick, etc.

wallet
small folding case for banknotes, etc.

wander
to travel about aimlessly; to meander; not to concentrate on the subject in hand
wanderer

want
(to) desire; (to) need; (to) lack
wanted wanting

war
(to engage in) armed fighting between countries
warlike warred warring wartime

ward
room in a hospital; administrative division of a town, etc.; child under the protection of a guardian or a court; to fend (off)

wardrobe
large cupboard for clothes; collection of clothes or costumes

warm
not hot or cold; having a moderate heat; friendly; generous; to make warm
warmer warmest warmly warmth

warn
to advise, esp. of future possible dangers
warning

warrant
authorization or justification; to justify; to assure
warrantable warrantor warranty warranties

warrior
fighter

was
singular of past tense of **be**
wasn't

wash
to clean with water; washing; thin coating of paint; rushing movement of waves behind a moving ship
washes washable

washing
clothes that need to be washed or that have been washed

waste
to use carelessly and inefficiently; rejected because no longer needed; waste material; to weaken
wastage wasteful wastefully wastefulness waster wasting

watch
to look at; to pay close attention to; to guard; small device that indicates the time
watches watcher watchful watchman

water
colourless odourless tasteless liquid that is a compound of hydrogen and oxygen; to sprinkle with water
watery

waterproof
(to make) impervious to water

wave
to move the hand from side to side as a greeting; moving ridge of water on the sea; curve; vibration conveying sound or light
wavier waviest waviness waving wavy

wax
smooth fatty substance produced by bees
waxes waxen waxiness waxy

way
course, method, or direction; road or path
ways

we
plural subject pronoun referring to the person who is speaking or writing and others

weak
not strong; fragile; diluted
weaken weaker weakest weakly weakness

wealth
large amount of money or riches; abundance
wealthier wealthiest wealthy

weapon
object used in fighting
weaponry

wear
to have as clothing on the body;
to become damaged by ordinary use
wearer wore worn

weary
(to make or become) tired
wearied wearier wearies weariest wearily weariness wearisome wearying

weather
conditions in the atmosphere as regards sunshine, rain, and wind; to make or become dry, discoloured, etc., through exposure to the air; to survive a storm, etc.

weave
to make a fabric by interlacing threads
weaver wove woven

web
network of threads spun by a spider; membrane joining the toes of some birds; the World Wide Web
webbed webbing web-footed

website
place on the Internet that stores information about a particular subject

wed
to marry
wedded or *wed wedding*

we'd
(*informal*) we had; we would

Wednesday
4th day of the week

weed
troublesome wild plant;
to remove weeds from
weedy

week
period of 7 days
weekday weekend weekly

weep
to shed tears
weeping weepy wept

weigh
to measure the weight of; to consider carefully; to raise anchor

weight
measure of heaviness; burden; influence or importance
weightier weightiest weightless weightlessness weighty

weird
strange; eerie; odd
weirdly weirdness

welcome
to greet in a friendly manner; received with pleasure
welcoming

welfare
good health, happiness and prosperity

well[1]
in a good way; favourably; in good health

well[2]
hole or shaft bored into the earth to reach a supply of water, oil, gas, etc.; source

we'll
(*informal*) we will

went
past tense of go

wept
past tense and past participle of **weep**

were
plural past tense of **be**
weren't

we're
(*informal*) we are

west
one of the 4 compass points; direction of sunset; opposite of east
westerly westward westwards

western
of or in the west; a film about cowboys, etc., in the western USA
westerner westernize or *westernise*

wet
moistened or covered with water; rainy; to make wet
wetted wetter wettest wetting

we've
(*informal*) we have

whale
(to hunt a) very large sea mammal valued esp. for blubber
whaler whaling

what
used to ask about the identity, nature, etc., of a person or thing

whatever
no matter what

wheat
kind of cereal grass, from whose grain flour is made

wheel
circular frame that turns on an axle; to turn on an axis

when
at what time; at the time at which

whenever
no matter when

where
to, at, or in what place; in the place in which

whereabouts
in what general area; general location

whereas
although

wherever
no matter where

whether
used to introduce the first of two or more alternatives

which
what (person or thing); and that

whichever
no matter which

while
(short) period of time; during the time that; although; to spend time pleasantly

whip
instrument with a lash for flogging; to flog with this; to beat eggs, cream, etc.
whipped whipping whippy

whisky
spirit distilled from fermented rye, barley, etc.
whiskies

whisper
(to utter in a) soft voice, not vibrating the vocal cords

whistle
(to make a) shrill piercing sound; device that produces a whistling sound
whistler whistling

white
colour of newly-fallen snow
whiten whiteness whiter whitest

who
what person or people
whoever

who'd
(*informal*) who had; who would

whole
not broken; complete; sound; unit; thing that is complete in itself
wholly

who'll
(*informal*) who will

whom
object form of **who**

who's
(*informal*) who is; who has

whose
of whom; of which

why
for what reason; reason
whys

wicked
bad or evil

wide
extending a long way from side to side
widely widen wider widest width

widespread
extensive; widely distributed

widow
woman whose husband has died, esp. one who has not remarried
widowed widower widowhood

width
measurement from one side to another; wideness
widths

wife
woman a man is married to
wives wifely

wild
not tame; savage; uncontrolled; stormy

will[1]
auxiliary verb used to express the future, firm intention, etc.
would

will[2]
mental faculty directing wishes, etc.; determination; to determine; written statement concerning disposal of property after death

willing
ready or inclined
willingly willingness

win
to come first in a competition; to gain a victory; to succeed
winner winning won

wind[1]
movement of air; air breathed; gas in the stomach or intestines
windward windy

wind[2]
to turn; to coil; to tighten (up)
winder wound

window
opening in a wall to provide light and air

wine
alcoholic drink made from fermented grape juice

wing
limb of a bird or insect used in flight; projecting support of an aircraft; side area of a playing-field; to fly
winged winger wingless

winter
season between autumn and spring
wintry or *wintery*

wipe
to clean or dry by rubbing with a cloth
wiper wiping

wire
thin flexible piece of metal; to install an electrical circuit in
wiring wiry

wisdom
knowledge and discernment

wise
having knowledge and discernment; prudent
wisely wiser wisest

wish
(to) desire
wishes wishful

with
by means of; having

withdraw
to take back; to remove; to retreat
withdrawal withdrawing withdrawn withdrew

withhold
to hold back; to keep back
withheld withholding

within
inside; not more than

without
not having

witness
person who gives evidence in a law-court; to see first hand
witnesses

woke
past tense of **wake**[1]

woken
past participle of **wake**[1]

wolf
wild flesh-eating dog-like animal; to eat greedily
wolves wolfed wolfing wolfish

woman
adult female human
women womanhood womanish womanly

won
past tense and past participle of **win**

wonder
feeling of surprise and awe; something marvellous; to feel wonder; to desire to know

wonderful
causing wonder; very good
wonderfully

won't
(*informal*) will not

wood
hard fibrous substance of which trees are made; group of trees, esp. one smaller than a forest
wooden woody

wool
fine soft hair from the fleece of sheep, goats, etc.
woollen (US *woolen*)

woolly
of or made of wool; woolly sweater; vague
woollies woollier woolliest woolliness

word
meaningful unit of sounds or letters; comment or message; promise; to express in words

wore
past tense of **wear**

work
effort (used to perform an activity); job; result of a process; to perform an activity; to function or operate

worker
person who works; employee

workshop
room or building where things are manufactured; period of practical instruction

world
earth, with all its inhabitants; human race
worldly

worldwide
in, across, or involving all countries of the world

worm
long thin invertebrate animal; to move very slowly

worn
past participle of wear

worry
to make or become troubled or anxious; trouble or anxiety; (of a dog) to shake or tear at something with its teeth
worries worried worrier worrying

worse
bad or ill to a greater degree
worsen

worship
(to take part in an) act of reverence offered to a deity; to adore; title used to address an official such as a mayor or magistrate
worshipful worshipped (US *worshiped*) *worshipper* (US *worshiper*) *worshipping* (US *worshiping*)

worst
bad or ill to the greatest degree; to defeat

worth
having a value of; deserving; value
worthless

worthwhile
worth the time and effort spent

worthy
deserving or honourable; worthy person
worthies worthier worthiest worthily worthiness

would
past tense of **will**[1] used to express a condition
would-be wouldn't

wound[1]
to injure the body; injury
wounded

wound[2]
past tense and past participle of **wind**[2]

wove
past tense of **weave**

woven
past participle of **weave**

wrap
to fold paper, cloth, etc., round something; shawl or cloak
wrapped wrapper wrapping

wreck
to damage severely; severely damaged remains, esp. of a ship at sea
wreckage wrecker wrecking

wrist
joint between the hand and the arm

write
to form letters, words, etc., on paper, esp. with a pen or pencil
writer writing written wrote

wrong
not right, correct, or true; unjust action; to treat unjustly
wrongdoer wrongdoing wrongful wrongfully wrongly

Xx

X-ray
photograph or examination
by a form of electromagnetic radiation
that can penetrate solids;
to treat, photograph,
or examine by means of X-rays
X-rays X-rayed X-raying

Yy

yacht
small sailing-boat
yachting yachtsman

yard
unit of length, 3 feet; long spar
on a mast to support a sail;
piece of enclosed ground

yawn
to open the mouth wide and breathe,
as when sleepy;
act of yawning

year
time taken by the earth to go once
round the sun; 12 months
yearly

yell
(to utter a) piercing loud cry

yellow
colour of butter; to make
or become yellow

yes
used to express agreement
or approval

yesterday
(on the) day before today; recent time

yet
up to this time; still; nevertheless

yield
to produce; result or amount
produced; to give way;
to surrender

you
subject and object pronoun referring to the person or people addressed; referring to people generally

you'd
(*informal*) you would; you had

you'll
(*informal*) you will

young
being in an early period of development
younger youngest youngish youngster

your
possessive form of you

you're
(*informal*) you are

yours
(the one or ones) belonging to you

yourself
reflexive form of you (singular)

yourselves
reflexive form of you (plural)

youth
quality of being young; young man; young people
youthful youthfully youthfulness

you've
(*informal*) you have

Zz

zero
symbol 0; nought; nothing
zeros or *zeroes*

zip
fastening device consisting of 2 toothed edges and a sliding interlocking tab
zipped zipper zipping zippy

zodiac
zone of the sky divided into 12 equal parts
zodiacal

zone
area or district; to arrange or divide into zones
zonal zoning

zoo
place where animals are kept
zoos

Section Notes

a
b
c
d
e
f
g
h
i
j
k
l
m
n
o
p
q
r
s
t
u
v
w
x
y
z

Section Notes